# "Essays to My Children"

*Preface to the Reader*

*Dedication to my Children*

1. ARE GOD THE FATHER, HIS SON ............Page 2
   JESUS CHRIST, AND THE HOLY GHOST
   THREE SEPARATE BEINGS?

2. IS GOD A SPIRIT? ..............................Page 10

3. THE APOSTASY AND THE RESTORATION....Page 18

4. OUR LIFE BEFORE OUR BIRTH ..............Page 30
   INTO MORTALITY

5. OUR HEAVENLY FATHER'S PLAN...........Page 42

6. THE OFFSPRING OF GOD......................Page 60

7. THE PRIESTHOOD OF GOD ..................Page 66

8. SALVATION FOR THE LIVING .............. Page 76
   AND THE DEAD

9. JESUS CHRIST IS JEHOVAH ................ Page 84

10. JUSTICE and PUNISHMENT..................Page 88
    MERCY and FORGIVENESS

**Duane Elias Thomas**
**667 SE Buck Gln**
**Lake City, FL 32025**

*Preface to Reader*

I am a member of the Church of Jesus Christ of Latter Day Saints. I was raised in the South, a native of rural north central Florida. I watched my parents, who were also members of the "Mormon" Church, patiently deal with the misconceptions about our faith held by many of our Bible believing Protestant neighbors. And I have learned that when discussing the beautiful truths of the restored gospel of Jesus Christ with my Bible believing friends, it is of great value to show where these simple truths, restored to the earth in these last days through a modern Prophet of God, were also taught by the Lord's prophets from the beginning of the world and are recorded in the Holy Bible.

In the fall of 2006 I received a phone call from one of my adult sons. His phone call was for help. One of his friends, who is not LDS, brought to him some questions about the Church that originated from a source antagonistic to the LDS Church. It is a sad fact to which we have become accustomed that some of the "misunderstandings" about the Church of Jesus Christ of Latter Day Saints have actually been promoted and perpetuated by some ministers of other faiths that seem to be threatened by the growth of the LDS Church and feel the need to propagate erroneous information about the Church in an attempt to deflect the public's curiosity or interest in listening to the message carried by our Missionaries. My son was simply not sure how he should respond. I asked my son to give me a few days and I would prepare some information and scriptures that he could use in responding to his friend's questions.

So, I sat down to write a brief explanation of what I as a member of The Church of Jesus Christ of Latter Day Saints actually believe on the particular subject, and to show how these beautiful truths are taught in the Bible. The more I wrote, the more I felt moved upon, and it became clear to me that all of my children, and my grandchildren, needed to understand the things that I was attempting to put down on paper. And even more importantly, I wanted them to know how to explain to someone that the doctrines of the Restored Gospel are not new, but that they have been taught by the Lord through his prophets from the very beginning. And most importantly,

I wanted my posterity to know, and to hear, and to see in my words my testimony and my witness to them as to the truthfulness of these teachings.

When I finished writing, I had written 10 essays. I compiled them and presented a personalized copy to each of my children and to each of my grandchildren as a gift from me.

As most of our children have left home for college or work or to start their own families, it has become increasingly difficult to touch and to influence their lives and especially the lives of our grandchildren. I want those I love most to know, on the record, what I, in my life time of study, have come to know as truth about who we are, where our origins lay, and what the real purpose of life is. I want my posterity to know where I stand and the grounds and principles upon which I have chosen to base my life.

With the encouragement of my family, I have decided to share these Essays in the hope that there may be others, both inside and outside the Church of Jesus Christ of Latter Day Saints, who are interested to see and understand that the doctrines of the restored gospel are not new, nor did they originate with Joseph Smith, but that these same truths have been taught by the Lord's anointed from the very beginning of the world, and are recorded in and documented by the Holy Bible.

With that in mind, I hope you will take these Essays in the spirit intended. I also refer you to the Holy Scriptures, both ancient and modern, as well as the words of the Lord's prophets in these days, and I encourage you to continue your study.

Sincerely,


Duane Elias Thomas

## Dedication to My Children

My dearest Children,

I was raised by pioneer parents, your grandparents, who not only taught me the gospel of Jesus Christ, but were absolute rocks of faithfulness all their lives. My example for you, I'm afraid, has not always been so unfailing. However, I have recently felt prompted to write down my thoughts and feelings in a way that I hope they may be a help to you in your life.

I have begun to set out here a few of the beautiful truths that I feel are so important for you to understand, truths taught by the prophets of the Lord from the beginning of the world, but lost for many hundreds of years after the death of the early apostles. As you know, these truths have been restored again as part of the "Restitution of all things..." promised by Peter as part of the events leading up to the Second Coming of our Lord.

I want each of my children and my grandchildren to understand the truth about God, and about who we are in relationship to Him. I hope these simple Essays will not only be a study guide for you, but an aid in helping you teach your children and those you love most about these precious truths.

I think these truths are self-evident. But in the event you have occasion to question these truths for yourself, I hope you will rely on my sure knowledge until you come to know of these things for yourself. From my lifetime of trying to learn all I can about these beautiful truths, I assure you, without any hesitation or doubt, that the things I've written here for you are true.

There is nothing original in these Essays, only those things I've learned from my study of the Holy Scriptures and from listening to and reading from prophets in our day, and things taught me through the Holy Spirit. These Essays simply reflect who I am, the truths on which I've chosen to base my life.

I pray that you will read and study these things while seeking the guidance of the Spirit of the Lord. He will, without question, guide you into all truth.

I hope these truths will be a foundation for your own life, that you may be an anchor for your own family and for the loved ones around you. It is the only way to true happiness.

I love you, my dear children, with all my heart. I expect great things of you in your life.

Dad

*Essay One*

## ARE GOD THE FATHER, HIS SON JESUS CHRIST, AND THE HOLY GHOST THREE SEPARATE BEINGS?

Perhaps the most disputed doctrinal question of the modern Christian era has been, and continues to be, "Are God the Father, the Son Jesus Christ, and the Holy Ghost the same being, or are they three separate and distinct individuals?" Unfortunately, the answer to the question is clouded, not by the scriptures themselves, but by the Council of Nicaea, a convocation of approximately 300 Christian Bishops from throughout the then known world, convened in 325 A.D. by the Emperor Constantine in the city of Nicaea in present day Turkey. Historical records place the number of Bishops present at the conference from 250 to 318 of approximately 1800 Bishops then existing. The Council was called by Constantine to supposedly resolve a major doctrinal dispute between Christian religious leaders of that day specifically on the above question. However, it appears the more likely reason the Emperor brought the conference together was to consolidate his own control and political domination over the Christian religious leaders throughout his empire.

The major action taken by the conference was a statement of doctrine as to the very question we are here discussing, i.e., the nature of Jesus in relationship to the Father; in particular, whether Jesus was of the same or merely of similar substance as God the Father. After a bitter and divided debate with those who believed that the Father and the Son were distinct beings, the conference issued its edict thereafter known as the "Nicene Creed" which stated, in essence, that the Father and the Son were the same substance or being. (See; The Council of Nicaea, Wikipedia, The Free Ency, *http://en.wikipedia.org/wiki/First_Council_of_Nicaea*)

After being revised somewhat in 381 A.D., this statement of belief became the accepted doctrine of the Roman and Eastern Orthodox Catholic Churches, and the source of all future reference on this topic, without further examination of the Holy

Scriptures themselves. The later Protestant sects that broke off from the Catholic Church largely took with them this same statement of belief, not based on the scriptures, but rather based on the Nicene Creed.

This background will help you understand the history behind and reasons for the present day belief of much of the Christian world on this topic. This essay, however, will look to the Holy Scriptures for guidance and teaching on the question, without regard to the Constantine dictated edict from the Council of Nicaea.

In examining the relationship between God the Father and his Son, Jesus Christ, one should first look at the natural conclusions drawn from reading the gospels, which document the life of our Lord. The natural and logical conclusions drawn from reading the words of Christ and of those who knew him most intimately, and from observing the actions of our Lord as he testifies that he is the Son of God, and as he repeatedly prays to and speaks of his Father, is that the relationship between Jesus and his Father is the same as the natural order of things would dictate, i.e., that the Father and the Son are two distinct individuals. It would otherwise be quite difficult to rationalize or explain away the fact that Christ so frequently prayed to his Father throughout the record of the gospels. Even during the most intense hours of his ordeal in the Garden of Gethsemane when he sweat great drops of blood from the agony of his sufferings in taking upon himself the sins of the world, Jesus sought his Father in prayer. Should we believe that Christ was simply praying to himself? It makes no sense to contemplate that Christ would have so consistently throughout his life perpetuated such an elaborate hoax on those he loved so dearly and to whom he sought to teach the truth.

The examination of a selected verse from the New Testament may provide some understandable basis for confusion in the mind of the casual and unstudied reader about this particular topic. John records the words of Jesus in responding to a question from a non-believer who confronted the Master with this question:

"...How long doest thou make us to doubt? If thou be the Christ, tell us plainly. Jesus answered them, I told you, and ye believed not: the works that I do in my Father's name, they bear witness of me. But ye believe not, because ye are not of my sheep, as I said unto you. My sheep hear my voice, and I know them, and they follow me: And I give unto them eternal life; and they shall never perish, neither shall any man pluck them out of my hand. <u>I and my Father are one.</u>" (John 10:24-30)

Christ says plainly that he and his Father are "one." A simple proffer of that verse alone by those seeking to support the Nicene statement that the Father and the Son are the same person might provide some rationale in the mind of the casual listener. Christ does not, however, say that he and his Father are the "same being". The attorney in me shouts to point out that there is a huge difference between saying we are "one," and saying we are the "same person." A husband and wife may, through their unselfish love and commitment to each other and to their marriage, become "one." But that does not mean they become the same person. They are still two separate individuals. What did Christ mean, then, by his statement that he and his Father are "one"?

To understand the true meaning of Jesus' statement that he and his Father are "one," we should look for reference to other discussions by Christ in the scriptures of being "one" with his Father. Specifically, the words of Jesus as he prayed to his Father at the conclusion of the Last Supper with his apostles (known as the Intercessory Prayer) just before he went out to the Garden of Gethsemane to begin his ordeal on the evening before his own crucifixion, as recorded by the Apostle John, are extremely enlightening.

**"I have glorified thee on the earth: I have finished the work which thou gavest me to do. And now, O Father, glorify thou me with thine own self with the glory which I had with thee before the world was. I have manifested thy name unto the men which thou gavest me out of the world: thine they were, and thou gavest them me; and they have kept thy**

word…. For I have given unto them the words which thou gavest me; and they have received them, and have known surely that I came out from thee, and they have believed that thou didst send me. I pray for them; I pray not for the world, but for them which thou hast given me; for they are thine. <u>And all mine are thine, and thine are mine; and I am glorified in them</u>. And now I am no more in the world, but these are in the world, and I come to thee. Holy Father, keep through thine own name those whom thou hast given me, <u>that they may be one, as we are</u>."

"Neither pray I for these alone, but for them also which shall believe on me through their word; <u>That they all may be one; as thou, Father, art in me, and I in thee, that they also may be one in us</u>; that the world may believe that thou hast sent me. <u>And the glory which thou gavest me I have given them; that they may be one, even as we are one; I in them, and thou in me, that they may be made perfect in one</u>; and that the world may know that thou hast sent me, and hast loved them, as thou hast loved me." (John 17: 4-11, 20-24)

Christ prays to the Father that his disciples, those given him out of the world by the Father, may be "one" as He and his Father are "one." In fact, Christ prays to the Father that not only His immediate disciples might be "one," but all those who shall, in the future, believe on Christ through the words of his disciples might also be "one" as He and his Father are one.

Now, it cannot be imagined here that Christ is praying to himself, asking himself to remake all of his present and future disciples into one single cosmic entity. Certainly not. Rather, it is exactly as it seems. Christ's prayer is to his Father, without any subterfuge, praying that all of his disciples may also be "one" in the same love and harmony and purpose as shared by he and his Father, that they may all be "one" just as he and his Father are "one"; that his disciples may ultimately "be made perfect in one" and share all things with he and his Father as joint heirs through Christ. (see also, Romans 8: 17)

Christ states in his prayer that all that is the Son's is also the Father's, and all that is the Father's is also the Son's. **"And all mine are thine, and thine are mine."** Christ said on another occasion that the Father hath given all things into the Son's hands. (John 3:35) Paul taught that the Father has appointed the Son "heir of all things." (Hebrews 1:2) Clearly, the Father has shared with the Son all that the Father has, i.e., "all things," including his power and his glory, his works and his purposes. The Father and the Son are one in possessions, in unity, in purpose, in harmony and in love. The Father's purposes and works are the Son's purposes and works. In this sense the Son and the Father are "one."

Therefore, in **John 10:30** when Jesus said, **"I and my Father are one"** what he was actually saying was that he and his Father share all things, and are completely united in love, in unity, and in purpose, which is what he was praying to be accomplished with his disciples in his Intercessory Prayer.

This doctrine of "oneness" was well known to the early Saints, and used frequently by the authors of the New Testament. Luke, in his book of Acts, speaks of the early members of the church at Jerusalem as "of one heart and of one soul."

**"And the multitude of them that believed <u>were of one heart and of one soul</u>: neither said any of them that ought of the things which he possessed was his own; but they had all things common."** (Acts 4: 32)

Paul, in his letter to the Galatians, says that the members of the church should all be "one" in Christ Jesus.

**"There is neither Jew nor Greek, there is neither bond nor free, there is neither male nor female: <u>for ye are all one in Christ Jesus</u>."** (Galatians 3: 28)

The Apostle John in his letter included in the New Testament as the First Epistle of John, seeks to clarify for the early Saints this very point about the heavenly order. He teaches that while the Father, the Son, and the Holy Ghost are three separate beings in heaven, they are never the less "one" in purpose, in love, and in harmony.

"For there are three that bear record in heaven, the Father, the Word, and the Holy Ghost: and these three are one." (1 John 5: 7)

Remember, the Apostle John is the author of this verse, and he is also the person who recorded the words of the great Intercessory Prayer uttered by Jesus at the conclusion of the Last Supper, as quoted above, in which the marvelous doctrine of being "one" with the Father and the Son is so eloquently expressed by Jesus. John is using in his letter the same language and concept of being "one" in teaching about the unity of love and purpose that exists among the Godhead as used by the Savior himself in his Intercessory Prayer in speaking about being "one" with his Father and with his disciples. We must, therefore, assume that John, in using the same language the Savior used in reference to the same topic, intended the same meaning given it by the Savior. There simply is no other possible conclusion.

As almost an after thought, it may be valuable to show the occasions documented in the New Testament when the presence of the Father, and the presence of the Son are demonstrated separately at the same time. At the time of Jesus' baptism, as recorded most carefully by Matthew, (Matthew 3:13-17) we see Christ being baptized by John the Baptist in the River Jordan, the Holy Ghost descending upon Christ like a dove, and the voice of the Father being heard introducing his Son with these words:

**"This is my beloved Son, in whom I am well pleased." (Matthew 3:17)**

Again, on the Mount of Transfiguration, (Matthew 17:1-9) when Moses and Elias appeared unto Christ with Peter, James, and John, his three chief apostles, as Jesus was transfigured before them, the voice of the Father was again heard introducing his Son.

**"While he yet spake, behold, a bright cloud overshadowed them: and behold a voice out of the cloud, which said, This is my beloved Son, in whom I am well pleased; hear ye him." (Matthew 17: 5)**

Recorded in Acts is the account of Stephen when he was about to be stoned by the Jews;

"But he, being full of the Holy Ghost, looked up stedfastly into heaven, and saw the glory of God, and Jesus standing on the right hand of God, and said, Behold, I see the heavens opened, and the Son of man standing on the right hand of God." (Acts 7:55-56)

How much more simple could it be said. Stephen, looking into heaven as he was full of the Holy Ghost, saw God the Father with Jesus Christ, the Son, standing on the right hand of the Father. He saw two men, not one.

Yes, the Father and the Son are two distinct beings as is amply and repeatedly testified to in the New Testament. However, as a consequence of the "falling away" or the "apostasy" foretold by the early Apostles that would occur after the death of the Apostles, the priesthood, or the authority Christ gave to his Apostles to act in his name, was lost; and many of the simple truths taught by the Savior and his Apostles, and understood by the early Saints, were lost. The world lay in a stupor of darkness for many centuries until the Lord again moved among the affairs of man to bring about the **"restitution of all things, which God hath spoken by the mouth of all his holy prophets since the world began"** (Acts 3:19-20) which Peter promised would occur before the long awaited glorious and triumphant Second Coming of our Lord Jesus Christ.

Ushering in this "restitution of all things" was the appearance of the Father and the Son to the boy Prophet Joseph Smith, clarifying immediately that the Father and the Son are two distinct individuals. Yes, as part of this great "restitution of all things" the simple truths of the gospel of Jesus Christ have again been restored to the earth through Prophets called in our day. Included among these glorious truths in beautiful clarity is the once again revealed knowledge that God the Father, and his Son, Jesus Christ, and the Holy Ghost are three separate and distinct individuals. They share all as the Godhead. They are one in complete unity of purpose and love and harmony. The Father's work and glory is also the work and glory of the Son and of the Holy Ghost.

The Savior's words to his prophet in these days affirming the correctness of this same doctrine of being "one" with the Father and the Son as he taught his disciples in the great Intercessory Prayer are found in the Doctrine and Covenants Section 35, verse 2.

**"I am Jesus Christ, the Son of God, who was crucified for the sins of the world, even as many as will believe on my name, that they may become the sons of God, even one in me as I am one in the Father, as the Father is one in me, that we may be one." (Doctrine and Covenants 35: 2)**

If you will ask your Father in heaven, in the name of his Son Jesus Christ, in humble prayer if these things are true, and if you will ask in sincerity and with real intent, with a burning desire to know, he will manifest the truth of these things to your mind and heart as surely as he has to mine. Of this I testify to you.

*Essay Two*

## IS GOD A SPIRIT?

One of the most misunderstood points of religious discussion, even among Christians, is the very nature of God. Is God merely a "spirit," or does he also have a body of flesh and bones? The confusion is not without basis since in the gospel of John in the New Testament we find:

**"God is a Spirit: and they that worship him must worship him in spirit and in truth."** (John 4:24)

However, a more expansive study of the New Testament teaches a far different conclusion than one gathers upon a cursory reading, by itself, of the above passage. So, what did Christ mean when he said the above verse recorded in John 4:24?

To understand Christ's meaning in John 4:24, let's examine Christ's words to Nicodemus when he taught Nicodemus that we all must be born of the water and of the Spirit to enter into the Kingdom of God (John 3:1-6). To be born of the water was clearly Christ's reference to baptism by water. To be born of the Spirit certainly was a reference to receiving the Gift of the Holy Ghost by the laying on of hands by those who had Christ's authority to do so, as taught so eloquently in the Acts of the Apostles. Christ concluded his words to Nicodemus with these:

**"That which is born of the flesh is flesh; and that which is born of the Spirit is spirit."** (John 3:6)

Accordingly, one realizes that with God, that which is "born of the Spirit," meaning born again of the Holy Ghost, becomes "spirit," or "spiritual," to God. Even the flesh is "spirit," or "spiritual" when born again of the Spirit. Therefore, as Christ instructed, we are to worship God in spirit (meaning, having been born again of the Holy Ghost) and in truth.

An eminently well-founded conclusion about the nature of God is drawn from observing the life of Jesus Christ, the Son, as recorded in the gospels. Studying Christ's life as a mortal, while understanding that at the same time he was the Son of

Almighty God, allows one to begin to comprehend the true nature of God, our Father in heaven. To understand the true nature of our Father in heaven, let us first understand the true nature of his Son, Jesus Christ.

In his earthly ministry Christ taught that he followed in his Father's footsteps, doing only what he had seen his father do. John recorded these words of our Master:

**"The Son can do nothing of himself, but what he seeth the Father do: for what things soever he** [meaning, The Father] **doeth, these also doeth the Son likewise." (John 5:19)**

Christ says that he only does those things that he has seen or that he sees his Father do. Clearly, we must conclude that Christ follows in his father's steps.

Christ's life and ministry as recorded in the gospels is clearly intended by our Lord as an example for us. Christ is our Great Exemplar. However, Christ taught us that our ultimate goal was to become **"perfect"** like our Father in heaven is **"perfect."**

**"Be ye therefore *perfect*, even as your Father which is in heaven is *perfect*." (Matthew 5:48)**

And as Christ is our Great Exemplar, we are to follow in Christ's footsteps as he follows in his Father's. So we look to Christ, the Son, to understand more about his Father.

At the end of Christ's ministry he fulfilled his foreordained mission to come to earth and to offer himself up as the ultimate sacrifice, the foreordained "lamb without blemish and without spot," and with his own precious blood he performed the infinite atonement for the sins of all mankind. **(See: 1 Peter 1:19-20)** On the cross, at the conclusion of his great work, Christ suffered physical death and his spirit left his physical body. Christ suffered mortal death on the cross voluntarily as part of his great mission. His physical body was then taken down from the cross and placed in a borrowed tomb. On the morning of the third day, as he had foretold, his spirit returned and entered again into his physical body, and as the Son of God he overcame mortal death by taking his life back up, resurrected in eternal glory, never to die again.

Very shortly after that glorious, momentous event, his beloved Mary Magdalene came to the garden tomb to finish her work of anointing the body of her Lord which she and others had begun as Christ's body was taken down from the cross and so hastily placed in the tomb on Friday afternoon before the start of the Jewish Sabbath at sundown. When she arrived, she found the great stone at the entrance of the tomb rolled away, and the tomb empty. As she wept, thinking someone had taken the body of her Lord, not yet understanding the great event that had transpired, Christ himself appeared to her. When she realized it was her Master she attempted to embrace him in joy and elation. However, Jesus forbade her from touching him at that time with these famous words:

**"...touch me not; for I am not yet ascended to my Father: but go to my brethren, and say unto them, I ascend unto my Father, and your Father; and to my God, and your God." (John 20:17)**

Mary hurried to tell the other disciples of what she had seen and heard, and on the evening of that same day, the disciples gathered themselves together in an upper chamber with the doors and windows shut out of fear of the Romans. As they excitedly spoke of what they had heard from Mary and others who had seen the risen Lord during the day, they still failed to grasp, as had Mary, the true nature of the resurrection. Luke records of this great occasion the following:

**"And as they thus spake, Jesus himself stood in the midst of them, and saith unto them, Peace be unto you. But they were terrified and affrighted, and supposed that they had seen a spirit. And he said unto them, Why are ye troubled: and why do thoughts arise in your hearts? Behold my hands and my feet, that it is I myself: handle me, and see; for a spirit hath not flesh and bones, as ye see me have. And when he had thus spoken, he shewed them his hands and his feet. And while they yet believed not for joy, and wondered, he said unto them, Have ye here any meat? And they gave him a piece of a broiled fish, and of an honeycomb. And he took it, and did eat before them." (Luke 24:36-43)**

We learn here very plainly that our spirit looks just like our physical body except without flesh and bones. We also learn that Christ, as the very first resurrected man, was not just a spirit but that he had a resurrected body of flesh and bones as well.

Christ wanted his disciples to clearly understand the nature of the event that had occurred. He wanted them to understand with perfect clarity that it was actually he, their Master, that had risen from the dead with his resurrected body of spirit and flesh and bones reunited and inseparably connected, never to die again. He was not just a spirit.

Christ wanted his disciples to clearly understand and record that the resurrection was literal, not some figurative slight of hand. He wanted his disciples to see, hear, touch and feel the reality of his resurrected body. He even wanted them to see and understand that he could eat and drink. And if there is one glorious truth from the New Testament that cannot be denied or misunderstood, it is that of the literal reality of the resurrection of our Lord Jesus Christ; that he broke the bands of physical, mortal death to live again in glory, never to die again.

After this event, our risen Lord remained with his disciples for approximately forty days, appearing unto many and giving additional teachings to his disciples who were now ready to understand more of his beautiful gospel truths. At the end of those forty days he took his apostles out onto the slopes of the Mount of Olives to the east of Jerusalem. And there, after giving them final instructions before his departure from them, he literally ascended up to heaven, as they watched. In the Book of Acts we read Luke's description of the occasion as follows:

"**And when he had spoken these things, while they beheld, he was taken up; and a cloud received him out of their sight. And while they looked stedfastly toward heaven as he went up, behold, two men stood by them in white apparel;**

**Which also said, Ye men of Galilee, why stand ye gazing up into heaven? <u>This same Jesus, which is taken up from you into heaven, shall so come in like manner as ye have seen him go into heaven.</u>**" (Acts 1:9-11)

We see the risen Lord, with the same resurrected body of flesh and bones that the disciples had touched and felt, as clearly recorded in the gospels, ascend up into heaven in the very presence of his apostles as the apostles watched. We then see two angels (men in white clothing) appear to the group as they watched their risen Lord ascend into heaven, who assured the apostles there present, that **"this *same* Jesus,** [*with this same resurrected never-to-die-again body of flesh and bone*] **which is taken up from you into heaven, shall so come in like manner as ye have seen him go into heaven."**

Can there be any dispute that the Lord Jesus Christ, the Son of God, where ever in the heavens he actually dwells today, is that same risen Lord with that same never-to-die-again resurrected body of flesh and bones as he had as he ascended into heaven from the presence of the apostles? I think not. Likewise, can there be any dispute that when our risen Lord and Savior returns again to earth in his gloriously triumphant second coming, that we will see him as the apostles of old saw him almost 2000 years ago from the slopes of the Mount of Olives as they watched him ascend into heaven, with that same never-to-die-again resurrected body of flesh and bones? Again, I think not.

The Apostle John in his first recorded epistle confirms that when Christ comes in glory at his second coming, we shall be like him.

**"Beloved, now are we the sons of God, and it doth not yet appear what we shall be: but we know that, when he shall appear, we shall be like him; for we shall see him as he is." (1 John 3: 2)**

So, if we have established that Jesus Christ, the Son of God, lives today as a resurrected man, with the same never-to-die-again resurrected body of flesh and bones as he took up with him into heaven almost 2000 years ago, we now must asked, "How is his Father?"

If we know how the Son is, can we draw a logical conclusion about how the Father is? I think we can. It is only logical that the offspring, or the Son, is like his Father. This is consistent with what Christ has said, that he does only those things that he has seen the Father do. (John 5:19)

The apostle Paul gives us some additional insight into the physical likeness of God the Father in the first chapter of Hebrews.

**"God** [*the Father*]...**hath in these last days spoken unto us by his Son**, whom he [*meaning, the Father*] **hath appointed heir of all things, by whom** [*meaning, by the Son*] **also he** [*meaning, the Father*] **made the worlds**; who [*meaning, the Son*] **being the brightness of his** [*meaning, the Father's*] **glory, and the express image of his** [*meaning, the Father's*] **person,..."** (Hebrews 1:1-3)

What Paul is telling us is that the Son is in the "express image" of his Father's "person." Or, in other words, Christ looks exactly like his Father. The Son looks exactly like the Father. Does this surprise us? Have you known a son who is the "spittin' image" of his Dad? That's how one might say it today. That's exactly what Paul is telling us. The Son's "person," or "body," is in the "express image," or "looks exactly like" the "person," or the "body" of the Father. The Son looks just like the Father. So, if we know that the Son has a glorious resurrected never-to-die-again body of flesh and bones, can we not conclude that the Father also is the same? In fact, they even look just alike.

As part of the **"restitution of all things which God hath spoken by the mouth of all his holy prophets since the world began,"** foretold by Peter to occur before the great and glorious second coming of our Lord Jesus Christ **(Acts 3:19-21)**, the Lord has revealed anew in this day, in brilliant simplicity, the truth about the true nature of God. The Lord, through his prophet, has taught us:

**"The Father has a body of flesh and bones as tangible as man's; the Son also; but the Holy Ghost has not a body of flesh and bones, but is a personage of Spirit. Were it not so, the Holy Ghost could not dwell in us." (D&C 130:22)**

These truths are beautiful, simple, logical and completely consistent with the teachings of the Old and New Testaments, and with the natural order of things. And they are confirmed by the teachings of the Lord's prophets called in theses last days. Further, and more importantly, the Holy Spirit testifies to my heart, my sweet children, that they are true.

*Essay Three*

## THE APOSTACY AND THE RESTORATION

From the beginning of the world, God has revealed truth to his children here on earth through prophets, men called by God, men to whom God spake and through whom he taught us, his children, the truth about God and about revealed religion.

**"Surely the Lord God will do nothing, but he revealeth his secret unto his servants the prophets." (Amos 3:7)**

Men such as Adam, Enoch, Noah, Abraham, Moses, and Peter were each called by God as a prophet in his own time. The Lord spoke to them and through them and revealed his truth to be taught to his children. Unfortunately, a pattern that has repeated itself from the days of Adam is that the people believed the prophet, for a time, and then usually turned away to their own wickedness. We see this repeatedly in the Old and the New Testament. We refer to this as a "falling away," or a period of *apostasy*. Without fail, after each period of apostasy, the Lord would again call another prophet to again restore and teach the people the truth about revealed religion. Although, we see at times in the Bible many hundreds of years pass from the time the people turned away from the Lord in apostasy until the Lord would call another prophet to once again restore and teach his truth. For example, many hundreds of years passed from the time the people turned away from the Lord during the ministry of Noah prior to the flood until the Lord called Abraham to once again establish his covenant with a righteous group of people; or from the days of Jeremiah when Jerusalem was destroyed by the Babylonians because of their wickedness until once again the Lord prepared a righteous John the Baptist to call his people to repentance and to prepare the way for the ministry our Lord Jesus Christ himself. The common tie throughout the religious history of the Bible after each episode of apostasy when the people turned away from the Lord to their own wicked ways is the calling by the Lord of a another Prophet through whom the Lord would restore and teach his truth to his people.

In the days of Jesus, we see that Jesus established his Church by calling twelve men he called Apostles, and giving them his power and authority to act in his name.

**"And he goeth up into a mountain, and calleth unto him whom he would: and they came unto him. And he *ordained* twelve, that they should be with him, and that he might send them forth to preach, and to have power to heal sicknesses, and to cast out devils:" (Mark 3:13-15)**

Christ selected twelve righteous men of his disciples and "ordained" them Apostles, meaning, he set them apart with a special calling and gave to them his power or his authority, which is called the Priesthood, so that they would be able to perform acts in his name, such as preach the gospel, heal the sick, cast out devils, and perform baptisms. This group of twelve Apostles, with the authority given them by Christ, would become the very foundation of Christ's church. Paul spoke of the importance of the Apostles in his epistle to the Ephesians.

**"Now therefore ye are no more strangers and foreigners, but fellowcitizens with the saints, and of the household of God; And are <u>built upon the foundation of the apostles and prophets, Jesus Christ himself being the chief corner stone;</u>" (Ephesians 2:19-20)**

Paul says the church is built on the foundation of the Apostles and prophets, with Jesus Christ himself as the chief corner stone.

Other priesthood officers were called in the early church such as, Elders, Seventies, Bishops, teachers, deacons, etc. But it was the Apostles who held the important calling of being the ones who held the *"keys"* and who were to authorize that the priesthood be given to others. (Matthew 16:19)

Paul, in the same letter to the Ephesians, discusses the importance of the Apostles and the other priesthood officers.

**"And he gave some, apostles; and some, prophets; and some, evangelists; and some, pastors and teachers;**

**<u>For the perfecting of the saints</u>, for the work of the ministry, for the edifying of the body of Christ:**

<u>**Till we all come in the unity of the faith**</u>**, and of the knowledge of the Son of God, unto a perfect man, unto the measure of the stature of the fullness of Christ:**

<u>**That we henceforth be no more children, tossed to and fro, and carried about with every wind of doctrine**</u>**, by the sleight of men, and cunning craftiness, whereby they lie in wait to deceive;"** (Ephesians 4:11-14)

Paul teaches that the Apostles and prophets, and the other priesthood offices, were a necessary part of Christ's Church for the **"perfecting of the saints;"** or in other words, to help the saints become perfect. Obviously, the Apostles and prophets, with their direct communication with God, could help the members of the church **"be no more like children, tossed to and fro, and carried about with every wind of doctrine,"** by the slight of hand of cunning men who lie in wait to deceive them.

The question is asked, will apostles and prophets and the other priesthood offices always be a necessary part of the true Church of Jesus Christ? Paul says they will be necessary **"Till we all come in the unity of the faith."** The thousands of different sects in the so called Christian world of today, each with their own different dogmas, is exactly the condition described by Paul as "children tossed to and fro and carried about with every wind of doctrine" that the foundation of apostles and prophets and other priesthood officers was intended to prevent. No, we haven't yet come to a **"unity of the faith."** Yes, we still need the heavenly guidance to be provided by the Lord through his apostles and prophets operating with his authentic priesthood authority.

Could a prophet, actually called of God, to whom has been given the priesthood of God as were the apostles of old, and with whom God communicates as he did with Peter or Moses of old, make a difference for us in the world today? Undoubtedly, yes! Is a true prophet called by God needed in the world today? Absolutely, yes!

Immediately after the ascension of our Lord from the Mount of Olives, as recorded in Acts 1:9-11, the disciples with the eleven remaining apostles (a total of one hundred and twenty in number) met in what was the first general conference of the church. Since maintaining the quorum of twelve apostles in tact was a critically important task, the first order of business of the first conference, with Peter conducting, was to select a new apostle to replace Judas. The method of the selection is worthy of some scrutiny. Luke records in **Acts 1:21-26;**

**"Wherefore of these men which have companied with us all the time that the Lord Jesus went in and out among us, beginning from the baptism of John, unto that same day that he was taken up from us, must one be ordained to be a witness with us of his resurrection. And they appointed two, Joseph called Barsabas,...and Matthias. And they prayed, and said, Thou, Lord, which knowest the hearts of all men, shew whether of these two thou hast chosen, that he may take part of this ministry and apostleship, ...And they gave forth their lots; and the lot fell upon Matthias; and he was numbered with the eleven apostles."** (Acts 1:21-26)

We see from this account that the apostles attempted to maintain the group or quorum of twelve apostles. From the account of this first conference we see the method used to select the first replacement apostle. The group sought the Lord's guidance in humble prayer before each of them indicated the name of the person whom they felt prompted by the Holy Spirit to select.

As other of the apostles were killed, we see others called in an attempt to keep the quorum of twelve apostles intact. From history we know that eventually the apostles all met with death at the hands of wicked men (with the exception of John). In the end, they were not only unable to maintain their quorum of twelve apostles, but were all killed. When the foundation of a building is snatched from under the building, what happens to the building? It falls, of course. And this is precisely what happened to the early church. When the apostles, who were the foundation of the church, and who held the apostolic calling which included the authority of Jesus Christ to act in his name (the Priesthood), which was necessary to carry on his work, were lost, the simple church of Jesus Christ was also lost. Most importantly, the priesthood authority given by Christ to the apostles, the authority to act in the name of Jesus Christ, was lost.

One might rightfully ask, "How can this be? How could the true church of Jesus Christ be lost?" The short answer is that the apostles not only knew this "falling away" would happen, they predicted it.

Paul was the most vocal in his writings in predicting what would happen after the apostles were gone. Paul taught that after he was gone, "grievous wolves" would enter in among the church, not sparing the flock.

**"For I know this, that after my departing shall grievous wolves enter in among you, not sparing the flock. Also of your own selves shall men arise, speaking perverse things, to draw away disciples after them." (Acts 20:29-30)**

In 2$^{nd}$ Timothy, Paul expounded further about this falling away which would come:

**"For the time will come when they will not endure sound doctrine; but after their own lusts shall they heap to themselves teachers, having itching ears; And they shall turn away their ears from the truth, and shall be turned unto fables." (2 Timothy 4:3-4)**

Paul, in his second letter to the Thessalonians gave perhaps the clearest prediction about the "falling away" or the apostasy. One of the most commonly accepted beliefs among the early Christians was that Jesus would return in glory, his Second Coming, as had been so clearly predicted. However, some of the Thessalonian saints apparently thought that the Second Coming would be soon. Paul takes the opportunity to correct their error about the Lord's Second Coming, and to also teach them about the impending "falling away" that must come first before the day of the Second Coming of our Lord.

**"That ye be not soon shaken in mind, or be troubled, neither by spirit, nor by word, nor by letter as from us, as that the day of Christ is at hand. Let no man deceive you by any means: for <u>that day shall not come, except there come a <i>falling away</i> first</u>, and that man of sin be revealed, the son of perdition;" (2 Thessalonians 2: 2-3)**

Paul teaches very plainly that *before* the Second Coming of our Lord there must first come a "falling away." The Spanish word used in the Spanish Bible for "falling away" in this verse in Thessalonians is "apostacia," which literally translated is "apostasy." Clearly, the falling away, or apostasy that would occur after the departure of the apostles and before the Second Coming of our Lord was both known and foretold by the early apostles.

The Apostle John, the last surviving apostle, had already begun to see the signs of what Paul had so boldly predicted. In the epistle of first John he writes:

**"And every spirit that confesseth not that Jesus Christ is come in the flesh is not of God: and this is that spirit of antichrist, whereof ye have heard that it should come; and even now already is it in the world." (John 4:3)**

Could John be more clear in what he was saying? In the Second Epistle of John he comments:

**"For many deceivers are entered into the world, who confess not that Jesus Christ is come in the flesh. This is a deceiver and an anti-christ." (2 John 1: 7)**

In John's third epistle, he points out some of the activity that exemplified the "grievous wolves" spoken of by Paul, and the spirit of the anti-christ spoken of earlier by John himself.

**"I wrote unto the church: but Diotrephes, who loveth to have the preeminence among them, received us not. Wherefore, if I come, I will remember his deeds which he doeth, prating against us with malicious words: and not content therewith, neither doth he himself receive the brethren, and forbiddeth them that would, and casteth them out of the church." (3 John 1: 9-10)**

Jude, the brother of James, in his epistle also documents the events that had been predicted by Paul which were already happening.

**"For there are certain men crept in unawares, who were before of old ordained to this condemnation, ungodly men, turning the grace of our God into lasciviousness, and**

denying the only Lord God, and our Lord Jesus Christ." (Jude 1: 4)

The Prophet Amos foresaw this period of apostasy, which was truly an era of darkness on the earth:

"Behold, the days come, saith the Lord God, that I will send a famine in the land, not a famine of bread, nor a thirst for water, but of hearing the words of the Lord: And they shall wander from sea to sea, and from the north even to the east, they shall run to and fro to seek the word of the Lord, and shall not find it." (Amos 8: 11-12)

While Paul foretold the "falling away" or the apostasy after the departure of the apostles and before the Second Coming of Christ, Peter promised that before the Second Coming, the Lord would again restore the gospel to the earth.

"**And he shall send Jesus Christ, which before was preached unto you: Whom the heaven must receive until the times of** *restitution of all things, which God hath spoken by the mouth of all his holy prophets since the world began.*" (Acts 3:20-21)

Peter speaks of the time when Jesus Christ will be sent again to the earth. But Peter says that before that day may come, there must first be a **"restitution of all things which God hath spoken by the mouth of all his holy prophets since the world began;"** all of it. All revealed truth spoken by God through the mouth of all his holy prophets since the world began will be restored. Peter promises a great restoration of gospel truth by God to the earth before the Second Coming of the Savior.

The Apostle John saw this great restoration of the gospel to be accomplished in the last days before the Second Coming of the Lord and recorded the vision in his Book of Revelation:

**"And I saw another angel fly in the midst of heaven, having the everlasting gospel to preach unto them that dwell on the earth, and to every nation, and kindred, and tongue, and people, saying with a loud voice, Fear God, and give glory to him; for the hour of his judgment is come..."** (Revelation 14: 6-7)

The Prophet Micah in Old Testament times saw the day of this great restoration and recorded in his book of **Micah 4:1-2;**

**"But in the last days it shall come to pass, that the mountain of the house of the Lord shall be established in the top of the mountains, and it shall be exalted above the hills; and people shall flow unto it.**

**And many nations shall come, and say, Come, and let us go up to the mountain of the Lord, and to the house of the God of Jacob; and he will teach us of his ways, and we will walk in his paths: for the law shall go forth of Zion, and the word of the Lord from Jerusalem."**

Daniel of old saw the day of this great restoration of the gospel to the earth and the establishment of the Church and Kingdom of God on the earth. He saw a stone, cut out of the mountain without hands, which rolled forth and brake into pieces the kingdoms of the world until it became a great mountain and filled the whole earth. (Daniel 2: 34-35)

**"And in the days of these kings shall the God of heaven set up a kingdom, which shall never be destroyed: and the kingdom shall not be left to other people, but it shall break in pieces and consume all these kingdoms, and it shall stand for ever." (Daniel 2: 44)**

In fact, after each period of apostasy from the days of Adam, God has called a new prophet through whom to again reveal his truth and to teach his gospel truths to his children here on earth. Should this surprise us that Peter says he will do it again? Not at all. And if God is going to do such a great work of restoration of everything he has spoken by his holy prophets since the beginning of the world, how will he do it? That's right! He will do it through a prophet to be called by Him for that purpose. And that's exactly what he did.

In the year 1820 in upper state New York, a young boy of 14 years old named Joseph Smith, along with his family, was in the midst of a great movement of religious fervor in their community. The various religious sects in the area were each striving for converts by claiming to have the truth. Yet each of the churches taught different doctrines. The young boy Joseph was a student of the Bible and wanted to join himself to a church, but was bewildered by the claims of the various churches to each have the truth while each was teaching a different doctrine. Joseph knew that there could only be one truth, and wanted sincerely to find the church which was right. He had about given himself up for despair when one day while reading in the epistle of James in the New Testament he read:

**"If any of you lack wisdom, let him ask of God, that giveth to all men liberally, and upbraideth not; and it shall be given him. But let him ask in faith, nothing waivering." (James 1: 5-6)**

These words struck Joseph's soul with more impact than any had ever done before. He knew he certainly needed wisdom. For without it, he would never be able to determine for himself which church he should join. So after much contemplation he decided to do exactly what the scripture in James instructed, to ask God. On a spring morning in 1820, the young Joseph retired to a previously selected secluded grove of trees and there, on his knees, he offered up his heart in prayer. No sooner had he begun than a dark force gathered about him and seized him so as to bind his tongue. As he persisted in attempting to call on God, he saw a column of light directly over his head, brighter he said than anything he had ever before seen, brighter than the noon day sun. This column of light gradually descended until it fell upon him and the dark force that had seized him was immediately gone. He said that within the light he saw two personages above him in the air. One of them called him by name and pointing to the other said, "Joseph, this is my Beloved Son. Hear him." No sooner had he collected his wits about himself than he asked the question he had come to ask, that is, which of the churches was true, and which should he join. He was told to join none of them. The Being who spoke to him told him that the churches taught for doctrine the teachings of man; that they drew near him with their mouths but their hearts were far from him. And many other things was Joseph told. Joseph was told that if he would be faithful, he would be an instrument in the Lord's hands to restore the true church of Jesus Christ to the earth. (see, Joseph Smith History, Pearl of Great Price, pgs 47-59)

God, the Father, and his Son Jesus Christ have again appeared to a chosen prophet on the earth! The voice of the Father, introducing his Son to man on the earth, has been heard again. The "restitution of all things" spoken of by the Apostle Peter of old has been ushered in by the appearance of our Lord Jesus Christ himself and his Eternal Father, Almighty God, to a prophet called by the Lord himself for that very purpose. The darkness has been pierced. Truth has again been revealed from heaven.

The chronology of events that transpired over the years that followed was exciting indeed. A messenger from God, a resurrected prophet of God who had lived here in the America's over 1400 years earlier, was sent from the presence of God to reveal to the young prophet Joseph Smith an ancient record, engraven on plates of gold, that contained the religious history of an ancient people who lived here in the Americas, written by the hand of Prophets of God who had lived among these people, and which contained an account of a visit of our Lord Jesus Christ to these people after his resurrection in the old world. The record had been hidden in the ground, waiting to come forth at a time designated by the Lord to bring to the world another testimony of the divinity of the Lord Jesus Christ, the Son of God, the Savior of the world. The record was eventually delivered to the young prophet Joseph with the direction to translate the record by the power of God. The record is called the Book of Mormon, named after a prophet who lived here in the Americas and who was instrumental in compiling the record contained on the plates of gold. The book contains the fullness of the gospel of Jesus Christ, and testifies that Jesus Christ is the Son of God, the Savior of the world, and is a second witness of Jesus Christ along with the Bible. (see, Joseph Smith History, Pearl of Great Price, pgs 47-59)

Part of this great **"restitution of all things"** was the restoration of the priesthood, or the authority to act in the name of Jesus Christ. Messengers from God were sent to the earth to personally confer upon Joseph Smith and his companion, Oliver Cowdrey, the Priesthood of Aaron, that is, the authority that John the Baptist had to baptize the Savior himself, and the higher Melchizedec priesthood given by Christ himself to the apostles of old. With this authority the prophet Joseph was directed by the Lord to reorganize the true church of Jesus Christ on the earth again, with a foundation of twelve apostles and all the other priesthood offices as in the primitive church.

The true Church of Jesus Christ is on the earth again after being lost for all those hundreds of years. Prophets of God have again been called by God on earth. The heavens are again open and light and knowledge again flow from the presence of God to enlighten and bless the lives of his children here on earth. The priesthood of God, with the authority to baptize and perform the other saving ordinances of the gospel is again on the earth.

The events and truths I've described here are momentous indeed. The only way for you to know if they are actually true is to study and learn of these truths for yourself, and to ask God, the Eternal Father, in the name of his Son Jesus Christ if these things are true. And if you will ask with real intent, having faith in Christ, he will reveal the truth of these things to your heart and soul by the power of the Holy Ghost. And by the power of the Holy Ghost, you may know the truth of all things. (Moroni 10: 4-5; John 16: 13)

I bear my own witness to you, my sweet children, that these things are true.

## Essay Four

## OUR LIFE BEFORE OUR BIRTH INTO MORTALITY

The question "Where do we come from?" has confronted us all. Without exception, all have been prompted to ask themselves, "Did I live before my birth into mortality?" Some have concluded that life begins with conception in our mother's womb. However, a study of Holy Scripture reveals there is much more to man's history than his life here on earth.

According to the Holy Bible, each of us are made up of a physical body of flesh and bones, as well as a spirit body that is the very essence of who we are, and that looks just like our physical body, except without flesh and bones. Paul, in his letter to the Hebrews, spoke of "the fathers of our flesh" and "the Father of our spirits."

**"Furthermore we have had <u>fathers of our flesh</u> which corrected us, and we gave them reverence: shall we not much rather be in subjection unto <u>the Father of spirits</u>, and live?" (Hebrews 12:9)**

Who are the "fathers of our flesh"? The fathers of our earthly bodies of flesh and bones are our own earthly fathers. Who is "the Father of spirits"? He is God, the Father of all of our spirits.

Clearly, God is the Father of all of our spirits, and in the very real sense, we are therefore all brothers and sisters. God is likewise the Father of Christ's spirit; and therefore, Christ is also our brother. The difference between Jesus and the rest of us is that the father of Christ's earthly body was no mere mortal man. Christ's father was not Joseph, but rather, as Christ frequently stated, was God the Father. So, God, the Father, was literally the Father of Jesus' earthly body of flesh, and also the father of Jesus' spirit body. Accordingly, Christ is referred to in the New Testament as "the only begotten of the Father," (see, John 1:14) meaning, the only begotten in the flesh. He is also referred to as the "Firstborn," (see, Hebrews 1:6; 12:23), meaning, the firstborn in the spirit.

That Christ is our sibling, our brother, was clearly taught by Christ in his encounter with Mary Magdalene in the early morning of the first day of his resurrection. Christ was crucified on the cross, and at the conclusion of his ordeal, his spirit left his physical body and he suffered mortal death. His physical body was then placed in the garden tomb, and on the morning of the third day his spirit came back into his body and he was literally resurrected, spirit and flesh inseparably reunited, never to be separated again, never to die again. When Christ appeared to Mary Magdalene in the early morning hours of that first day of his resurrection, Mary attempted to embrace her Lord, but Christ forbade her at that time with these famous words:

**"Jesus saith unto her, Touch me not; for I am not yet ascended to my Father; but go to my brethren, and say unto them, I ascend unto my Father, and your Father; and to my God, and your God." (John 20:17)**

Clearly, Christ is our brother in the sense that God is the father of all our spirits, including Jesus' spirit.

We learn more about a spirit, as well about the literal reality of the resurrection, from an incident recorded by Luke that occurred on the evening of the first day of Christ's resurrection. The disciples had heard from Mary and others that they had seen the risen Christ, that he was alive. That they did not fully understand what had happened is abundantly clear. The disciples had gathered in an upper chamber with the doors and windows shut out of fear of the Romans. And as they excitedly spoke of the things they'd heard, Christ himself appeared in their midst.

**"And as they thus spake, Jesus himself stood in the midst of them, and saith unto them, Peace be unto you. But they were terrified and affrighted, and supposed that they had seen a spirit. And he said unto them, Why are ye troubled? And why do thoughts arise in your hearts? Behold my hands and my feet, that it is I myself: handle me, and see; for a spirit hath not flesh and bones, as ye see me have. And when he had thus spoken, he shewed them his hands and his feet. And while they yet believed not for joy, and wondered, he said unto them, Have ye here any meat? And they gave**

him a piece of a broiled fish, and of an honeycomb. And he took, and did eat before them." (Luke 24:36-43)

We learn from this incident that a spirit looks just like a person, except without a body of flesh and bones. We also learn of the reality of the resurrection. Christ wanted his disciples to understand clearly the nature of the resurrection, and the nature of a resurrected being. He had them touch his hands and his feet for them to understand with absolute certainty that he had a body of flesh and bones, resurrected from the tomb, never to die again. He was not just a spirit.

So we each have within us a spirit which is the very essence of who we are. We know when our physical body was born as each of has our own birth date. But the next question is not so readily answered by the Christian world of today. **"WHEN WERE OUR SPIRITS BIRTHED?"**

First, let us consider when the spirit of our brother, Jesus Christ, was birthed. We learn from the gospel of John that Christ has existed from the beginning with the Father. John refers to Jesus, the Son, as "the Word" in the beautiful passage in the first verses of his recorded gospel.

**"In the beginning was the Word, and the Word was with God, and the Word was God. The same was in the beginning with God. All things were made by him; and without him was not any thing made that was made.... And the Word was made flesh, and dwelt among us, (and we beheld his glory, the glory as of the only begotten of the Father,) full of grace and truth." (John 1:1-3, 14)**

John teaches that Christ, the Word, "was," meaning that he existed, "in the beginning," and that he was with God, or the Father, "in the beginning." Now the usage of the term, "the beginning," does not necessarily mean there was a start date that marked the beginning of things, but rather it means that God, who has existed from everlasting to everlasting (or, forever into the past), has had with him, from the very beginning, Christ, meaning that Christ has also existed with the Father forever.

Paul refers to Christ as **"the Firstbegotten" (Hebrews 1:6)** and as **"the Firstborn" (Hebrews 12:23)**. John refers to

Christ as **"the beginning of the creation of God" (Revelation 3:14).** Clearly, the New Testament teaches that Jesus Christ was the Firstborn of the Father's spirit offspring, and as such he is our eldest brother.

As additional confirmation from the Bible of Christ's premortal existence with the Father, consider the following. We know that Christ, who was then still a spirit, was selected and foreordained by the Father at a time before the foundation of the world, (i.e., before the earth was created) to come to earth at his designated time and to be sacrificed as the ultimate lamb without blemish and without spot, and with his own precious blood to perform the infinite atonement for the sins of all of us, his younger brothers and sisters. This mission of Jesus Christ to be the Savior of the world was the very heart of Father's plan for his spirit children. Peter understood and taught this great truth in **1 Peter 1:19-20.**

**"But with the precious blood of Christ, as of a lamb without blemish and without spot: Who verily was foreordained before the foundation of the world, but was manifest in these last times for you."**

John the Revelator, the Apostle whom Jesus loved, and the author of the Book of Revelation, also taught this same principle, that Christ's mission as the Savior of the world, though fulfilled or accomplished in the meridian of time during Christ's earthly ministry, was none the less given Him from before the foundation of the world was laid, and was efficacious for all who lived from the beginning of the world, not just for those who came after Him. John refers to Christ as **"the Lamb slain from the foundation of the world." (Revelation 13:8)**

In his great Intercessory Prayer after the last Passover supper with his apostles and before he went out to begin his ordeal in the Garden of Gethsemane, Christ prayed to his Father:

**"I have glorified thee on the earth: I have finished the work which thou gavest me to do. And now, O Father, glorify thou me with thine own self with the glory which I had with thee before the world was....for thou lovedst me before the foundation of the world." (John 17:4-5, 24)**

So, if we understand that Christ's spirit was created or birthed by our Father an infinitely long period of time ago, and that Christ lived as a Spirit with the Father for an infinitely long period of time before his mortal birth here on the earth, the next question to be asked is, **"When were *our* spirits birthed or created?"**

The short answer is that the Bible teaches abundantly that we also were created, or birthed, and lived with our Father in heaven as his spirit children long before our birth into mortality. Here are a few of the places it so teaches.

The Lord told Jeremiah that:

**"Before I formed thee in the belly I knew thee; and before thou camest forth out of the womb I sanctified thee, and I ordained thee a prophet unto the nations." (Jeremiah 1:5-6)**

We learn here that Jeremiah both lived and was known by the Lord while he was yet a spirit before his earthly body of flesh and bones was ever formed in the belly of his mortal mother. We also learn that Jeremiah obviously had his own moral agency to make choices for himself, and that he made righteous choices in his premortal life for the Lord to know of his righteousness, even before his birth into mortality, and to foreordain him while he was still a spirit to be a prophet here in mortality.

Paul, (we learn from his letter to the Ephesians), also understood and taught that we all both lived and made choices before we were born into mortality, before the world was created, so as to demonstrate our righteousness to the Lord, so as to be chosen in him before the foundation of the world, even as was Jeremiah.

**"According as he hath chosen us in him before the foundation of the world, that we should be holy and without blame before him in love:" (Ephesians 1:4)**

In chapter 9 of the gospel of John, verses 1 and 2, we read of a very interesting occasion in which a man who was born blind was brought to Jesus by his disciples with the question: **"Master, who did sin, this man, or his parents, that he was born blind?" (John 9: 1-2)**

The answer to the question is not the point of this story, but rather the question itself reveals the lesson to be learned. What we learn here is about the understanding of Christ's disciples concerning the nature of our lives before our birth into mortality. The only way for the man, who was born blind, to have sinned so as to be the cause of his own blindness from birth, would be for the man to have sinned before he was born. This was obviously a possibility in the minds of the disciples as they understood that we lived as spirits with our Father in heaven before our birth into mortality, and that we had our own agency to choose for ourselves, even then.

Consider the first chapter of Genesis which is the summary of the six creative periods, culminating with the creation of man and woman in the image and likeness of God.

**"And God said, Let us make man in our image, after our likeness:...So God created man in his own image, in the image of God created he him; male and female created he them." (Genesis 1:26-27)**

Then, after the conclusion of the six creative periods, when the work of the creation is completed, we find, in the beginning of the 2$^{nd}$ Chapter of Genesis, that God rested on the seventh day, and blessed the seventh day, **"because that in it he had rested from all his work which God created and made."** Then, verse 4 of Chapter 2 goes on to speak of the "generations" of the heavens and the earth, that is, to refer back to the six creative periods described in Chapter 1, and the seventh, during which God rested, and then goes on to explain something very, very interesting.

**"These are the generations of the heavens and of the earth when they were created, in the day that the Lord God made the earth and the heavens, and every plant of the field before it was in the earth, and every herb of the field before it grew: for the Lord God had not caused it to rain upon the earth, and there was no man to till the ground." (Genesis 2:4-5)**

Consider this carefully. We read in the 1$^{st}$ chapter of Genesis of the creation of all the things that would eventually go into the earth, the plants, the insects, the birds, the fishes, the animals, as well as man and woman. But in verse 4 of the very next chapter we read that God **"created...every plant of the field before it was in the earth, and every herb of the field before it grew,"** and even though the creation of both man and woman was described in Chapter 1, Chapter 2 of Genesis then says **"there was no man yet to till the ground."** Man and woman were created but there was no man yet to till the ground in the earth. What does this mean? What it means is that they were all created before they were placed in the earth. And how were they then created? They were created spiritually in heaven before they were created physically in the earth, all plant and animal life as well as all of us spirit children of God. We were all created first spiritually before the foundation or creation of the world, before we were created physically here in the earth.

That this is the correct understanding from Genesis of the creation is confirmed to us by the Lord through his prophets in these last days. In the book of Moses from the Pearl of Great Price we read the following more complete rendition of Moses' original writings of this passage:

**"And now, behold, I say unto you, that these are the generations of the heaven and of the earth, when they were created, in the day that I, the Lord God, made the heaven and the earth, and every plant of the field before it was in the earth, and every herb of the field before it grew. For I, the Lord God, created all things, of which I have spoken, spiritually, before they were naturally upon the face of the earth. And I, the Lord God, had created all the children of men; and not yet a man to till the ground; for in heaven created I them; and there was not yet flesh upon the earth, neither in the water, neither in the air;"** (Moses 2:4-5)

The wise and great Solomon who wrote, among other things, the book of Proverbs was blessed by the Lord with great wisdom and knowledge. In speaking of "wisdom" in Chapter 8 of Proverbs, verses 22-31, Solomon teaches that the Lord possessed wisdom **"in the beginning," "from everlasting," "from the beginning," "or ever the earth was."** He goes to great lengths here to describe the time before the world was created, and speaking as if giving words to "wisdom" itself he says:

"**When there were no depths,... before the mountains were settled,... while as yet he had not made the earth, nor the fields, nor the highest part of the dust of the world, ...when he prepared the heavens,... when he appointed the foundations of the earth,...my delights were with the sons of men.**" (Proverbs 8:24-31)

Solomon understood this great truth that the sons of men were there already with God before the world was created. Solomon understood that the children of men were born as spirit children of our Father in heaven before the world was ever created, and that we lived with him an infinitely long period of time, learning wisdom from him and growing.

Teaching these same great truths in a revelation given through the Prophet Joseph Smith on May 6, 1833, the Lord Jesus Christ said:

"**And now, verily I say unto you, I was in the beginning with the Father, and am the Firstborn;**

"**Ye were also in the beginning with the Father;...**"(D&C 93:21,23)

He then went on to explain:

"**Man was also in the beginning with God. Intelligence, or the light of truth, was not created or made, neither indeed can be.**

**All truth is independent in that sphere in which God has placed it, to act for itself, as all intelligence also; otherwise there is no existence.**" (D&C 93:29-30)

Our birth as spirit children of our Father in heaven does not mean we were created out of nothing. In our spirit birth, our Father provided for us a spirit body (*a body not of flesh and bones, but never the less matter more fine and pure which can only be discerned by purer eyes*; see, D&C 131:7) within which to house our "Intelligence," the very essence of who we are. Our "Intelligence" is that part of us which has co-existed eternally with God.

Life as a spirit child of our Father in heaven, consisting of our Intelligence united within a spirit body of fine and pure matter, was our *first probationary estate*. It was the beginning of our progress toward becoming perfect like our Father. As an essential ingredient in our progress, Father assured for us our "agency" to act and choose for ourselves.

Jude spoke of those **"which kept not their first estate." (Jude 1:6)** They were those spirit children who chose to *not* follow Father's plan into mortality, but rather chose to follow Lucifer, and were cast out of heaven for rebellion. **(See, Revelation 12:7-9; Isaiah 14:12-16; Moses 4:1-4; Abraham 3:25-28)**

It was there, during our premortal life, that Father presented us with His great plan for his children to have the opportunity, or the "hope" as Paul said it, to progress and to grow to become more like him, the "hope" to have a life like our Father, and to share with Father and with his Firstborn son, Jesus, the ultimate blessing referred to often in the scriptures as "eternal life". The **"hope of eternal life" (Titus 1:2),** as Paul called this great plan of our Father's for us, included creating an earth for us to be able to come to in order to obtain a body of flesh and bones, like our Father's, and to be tried and tested to see if we would be obedient to Father's commandments, and for us to be able to develop our own faith. There simply was no other way. We had to experience the bad to be able to know and appreciate the good. To insure this, Father preserved for us our agency to choose for ourselves. And he promised to send a Savior, his own firstborn spirit son, to sacrifice his own precious blood in mortality to redeem us from our sins, if we would repent and follow his teachings. **(See, 1 Peter 1:19-20)**

As part of the **"restitution of all things which God hath spoken by the mouth of all his holy prophets since the world began" (Acts 3:20-21)** as promised by Peter to occur before the second coming of Christ, our Lord has shed more light for us on this great "Plan" of our Father's. A record of a vision shown by the Lord to Abraham concerning the presentation of this great plan to Father's spirit children, found in **Abraham 3:22-28** as restored in these last days as part of the Pearl of Great Price reveals:

"Now the Lord had shown unto me, Abraham, the intelligences that were organized before the world was; and among all these there were many of the noble and great ones; And God saw these souls that they were good, and he stood in the midst of them, and he said: These I will make my rulers; for he stood among those that were spirits, and he saw that they were good; and he said unto me: Abraham, thou art one of them; thou wast chosen before thou wast born. And there stood one among them that was like unto God, and he said unto those who were with him: We will go down, for there is space there, and we will take of these materials, and we will make an earth where on these may dwell; And we will prove them herewith, to see if they will do all things whatsoever the Lord their God shall command them; And they who keep their first estate shall be added upon; and they who keep not their first estate shall not have glory in the same kingdom with those who keep their first estate; and they who keep their second estate shall have glory added upon their heads for ever and ever. And the Lord said: Whom shall I send? And one answered like unto the Son of Man: Here am I, send me. And another answered and said: Here am I, send me. And the Lord said: I will send the first. And the second was angry, and kept not his first estate; and, at that day, many followed after him." (Abraham 3:22-28)

The announcement to us of this great plan of our Father in heaven for us must have been an occasion of great jubilation. We see a reference to this joyous occasion in the Book of Job, when the Lord was pointing out to Job how little Job knew or understood of the events that transpired when the earth was created.

"Where wast thou when I laid the foundations of the earth? Declare, if thou hast understanding. Who hath laid the measures thereof, if thou knowest? Or who hath stretched the line upon it? Whereupon are the foundations there fastened? Or who laid the corner stone thereof; <u>When the</u>

**morning stars sang together, and all the sons of God shouted for joy?" (Job 38:4-8)**

We certainly must have sang together and shouted for joy to see the foundations of the earth laid. For this meant we would soon be able to embark upon this great opportunity provided us by our Father to come to earth, to gain a physical body, and to participate in Father's plan for us to continue to grow and become more like him.

So the earth was created and the plan of our Father implemented, with Jesus Christ himself, our eldest brother, the firstborn of our Father in the spirit, and the only begotten son of the Father in the flesh, as the very heart and central figure of our "hope for eternal life."

These are beautiful, simple, unadulterated truths, revealed anew by the Lord to us in these last days, but which only confirm the truths taught by the prophets of old. Undeniably, these truths were included in their writings originally, and are still found in the translations of the Bible that have come down to us through history, albeit not expressed with such clarity and simplicity as penned by their original authors.

As you contemplate these simple truths and allow them to instill upon your soul, if you will open your heart to the Holy Spirit, the Spirit will whisper to your heart that these things are true, as it has to mine. Of this, my sweet children, I testify.

*Essay Five*

## OUR HEAVENLY FATHER'S PLAN

All of us were created or birthed spiritually in heaven as the offspring of God, our Father in heaven, before the foundations of the earth were laid. And we lived with Him in heaven as his children for an infinitely long period of time, and learned from him and grew in wisdom and knowledge to the extent possible for us as spirits without a body of flesh and bones. Even then, we exercised the agency given us by our Father to choose for ourselves to either follow Father's example and counsel, or not. (See, ESSAY FOUR: OUR LIFE BEFORE OUR BIRTH INTO MORTALITY, pg 30 supra)

During our premortal life with our Father, He presented to us his plan to give us the opportunity, or the "hope," (Titus 1:2) for us to become more like Him, who even then was an exalted glorious man with a never-to-die body of flesh and bones, and who had created us, his children, in his own image and likeness. (See, ESSAY TWO: IS GOD A SPIRIT?, pg 10 supra)

Father's plan for us included creating an earth for us where we could come to receive a physical body of flesh and bones, like His, and where we would have an opportunity to be tried and tested to exercise our own agency, to develop our own faith, and to see if we would be willing to obey Father's commandments outside his immediate presence in the face of trials and temptations.

Father knew that at the end of our mortal experience and probation here on earth we would suffer "**physical death,**" or the separation of our spirit from our body of flesh and bones. He also knew that because each of us would also commit sins here on earth we would be forever barred or excluded from returning to his presence, which is called "**spiritual death,**" since no unclean thing can enter into the presence of God. (See, Alma 42) Father therefore promised, as the central part of his plan of happiness for us, to send us a Savior, a mission he assigned to his Firstborn Son in the spirit, Jesus Christ, whom He foreordained to come to earth at the appointed time and to be, himself, sacrificed as the great and infinite atoning sacrifice, the ultimate lamb without blemish and without spot, to do something for us we couldn't do for ourselves, that is, to fulfill the demands of Justice, to overcome the effects of physical death for all mankind, and to take upon himself the punishment for our own sins so as to allow us to be washed clean from our sins, if we would repent and obey his commandments. (See, 1 Peter 1: 19-20) To be washed clean of our own sins is necessary to enable us to return to the presence of our Father and there become perfected like him. Without a Savior to redeem us, we would all be lost forever to the effects of both physical death and spiritual death. (See, 2 Nephi 9:6-15)

So, the world was created by the hand of Jesus, the firstborn of all our Father's spirit children, under the direction of Father (See, Hebrews 1). And Adam and Eve, our first parents, were placed in the Garden of Eden. Since our participation in Father's plan was always by our own choice, for Father's way is to never compel our obedience to his will, He made it necessary that Adam and Eve would actually have to choose the effects of mortality for both themselves and for their posterity after them. Also, since participation in Father's plan was a matter of choice, there were many of the spirit children of Father who, for their own reasons, chose not to follow Father's plan. These were Lucifer and his followers who were cast out of Father's presence for rebellion. (See, Revelation 12:7-9; Isaiah 14:12-16; Jude 1:6; Moses 4:1-4; Abraham 3:26-28; D&C 76:25-28; D&C 29:36-39)

In the Garden of Eden, Father gave Adam and Eve two commandments: (1) to multiply and replenish the earth; and (2) to *not* partake of the Forbidden Fruit. However, Father told Adam and Eve that it was nevertheless given unto them to choose for themselves, but to remember, that in the day that they should eat of the forbidden fruit, they should surely die. (Genesis 2:15-25; Moses 2-3)

Of course, partaking of the forbidden fruit was a choice Adam and Eve made after realizing that it must be so to fulfill Father's purposes and to allow their posterity the opportunity also to come to earth. (Moses 4) This choice of our first parents was clearly both brave and wise. Adam and Eve surely were great souls in their premortal life to have been chosen by our Father to perform this most critical and honored role here in mortality. Satan's actions in the Garden, certainly without his intention to do so, merely helped facilitate this great passage of Adam and Eve into mortality which made it possible for us, as their posterity, to follow them into first hand participation in this mortal phase of Father's plan for us.

The results of Adam and Eve's violation of Father's commandment in the Garden of Eden were two fold: (1) Adam and Eve became subject to ***physical death*** which came into the world because of their transgression. Before the "fall," brought on by Adam and Eve's transgression, there was no physical death in the world. However, a benefit of their transition into mortality was that it was now possible for Adam and Eve to have children which opened the door for us as their posterity to follow them into this mortal probation. (See, 2 Nephi 2:22-23) And, (2) Adam and Eve were expelled from the Garden of Eden and alienated from the presence of God, which is called ***spiritual death***, because of their transgression, for no unclean thing can abide in the presence of God. (Alma 42:9)

From the days of Adam and Eve, God taught his children to look forward to the great atoning sacrifice of his Son, Jesus Christ, the Promised Messiah, the Lamb of God, the Firstborn of the Father in the spirit, and the only begotten of the Father in the flesh, who would be born into mortality at his appointed time to literally be the Lamb without blemish and without spot, foreordained by the Father from before the foundation of the world as part of Father's great plan or "Hope of Eternal Life" (Titus 1:2) for his children, to atone, with his own precious blood, for the sins of all mankind. (1 Peter 1:19-20)

To teach his children here on earth about this great atoning sacrifice to be performed by the Lamb of God, God instructed his children, through his prophets, to offer up as a sacrifice to God the firstlings of their flocks, a male firstborn lamb without any blemish or spot. This sacrifice was to be done as a *similitude* of the offering of God's own Firstborn Son, Jesus

Christ, the only begotten of the Father in the flesh, the Messiah promised by the Father from before the foundation of the world, to be made to atone for the sins of all mankind. (See, Moses 5:6-8)

Over the millennia from the fall of Adam until the birth of Christ the righteous posterity of Adam and Eve looked forward to the coming of the Messiah, the Son of God, who would perform this most critical role in Father's plan. All of the Old Testament prophets prophesied of this great coming event. (See, Acts 10:43; John 5:39; John 5:46)

Isaiah wrote of the future birth of the Messiah in **Isaiah 9:6:**

**"For unto us a child is born, unto us a Son is given: and the government shall be upon his shoulder: and his name shall be called Wonderful, Counsellor, The mighty God, The everlasting Father, The Prince of Peace."** (Isaiah 9:6)

Isaiah described very beautifully and accurately the life and mission of the Savior.

**"For he shall grow up before him as a tender plant, and as a root out of a dry ground: he hath no form nor comeliness; and when we shall see him, there is no beauty that we should desire him.**

**He is despised and rejected of men; a man of sorrows, and acquainted with grief: and we hid as it were our faces from him; he was despised, and we esteemed him not.**

**Surely he hath borne our griefs, and carried our sorrows: yet we did esteem him stricken, smitten of God, and afflicted.**

**But he was wounded for our transgressions, he was bruised for our iniquities: the chastisement of our peace was upon him; and with his stripes we are healed.**

**All we like sheep have gone astray; we have turned every one to his own way; and the Lord hath laid on him the iniquity of us all.**

**He was oppressed, and he was afflicted, yet he opened not his mouth: he is brought as a lamb to the slaughter, and**

as a sheep before her shearers is dumb, so he opened not his mouth.

He was taken from prison and from judgment: and who shall declare his generation? For he was cut off out of the land of the living: for the transgression of my people was he stricken.

And he made his grave with the wicked, and with the rich in his death; because he had done no violence, neither was any deceit in his mouth.

Yet it pleased the Lord [*meaning, the Father*] to bruise him [*meaning, the Son*]; he hath put him to grief: When thou shalt make his soul an offering for sin, he shall see his seed, he shall prolong his days, and the pleasure of the Lord shall prosper in his hand.

He shall see of the travail of his soul, and shall be satisfied: by his knowledge shall my righteous servant justify many; for he shall bear their iniquities.

Therefore will I divide him a portion with the great, and he shall divide the spoil with the strong; because he hath poured out his soul unto death: and he was numbered with the transgressors; and he bare the sin of many, and made intercession for the transgressors." (Isaiah 53:2-12)

In the Americas, prophets of God here also taught of the future coming of the Messiah.

"For behold, the time cometh, and is not far distant, that with power, the Lord Omnipotent who reigneth, who was, and is from all eternity to all eternity, shall come down from heaven among the children of men, and shall dwell in a tabernacle of clay, and shall go forth amongst men, working mighty miracles, such as healing the sick, raising the dead, causing the lame to walk, the blind to receive their sight, and the deaf to hear, and curing all manner of diseases.

And he shall cast out devils, or the evil spirits which dwell in the hearts of the children of men.

And lo, he shall suffer temptations, and pain of body, hunger, thirst, and fatigue, even more than man can suffer, except it be unto death; for behold, blood cometh from every pore, so great shall be his anguish for the wickedness and the abominations of his people.

And he shall be called Jesus Christ, the Son of God, the Father of heaven and earth, the Creator of all things from the beginning; and his mother shall be called Mary.

And lo, he cometh unto his own, that salvation might come unto the children of men even through faith on his name; and even after all this they shall consider him a man, and say that he hath a devil, and shall scourge him, and shall crucify him.

And he shall rise the third day from the dead; and behold, he standeth to judge the world; and behold, all these things are done that a righteous judgment might come upon the children of men.

For behold, and also his blood atoneth for the sins of those who have fallen by the transgression of Adam, who have died not knowing the will of God concerning them, or who have ignorantly sinned.

But wo, wo unto him who knoweth that he rebelleth against God! For salvation cometh to none such except it be through repentance and faith on the Lord Jesus Christ."

"And moreover, I say unto you that there shall be no other name given nor any other way nor means whereby salvation can come unto the children of men, only in and through the name of Christ, the Lord Omnipotent." (Mosiah 3:5-12, 17)

The posterity of Adam, including each of us, find ourselves facing the certain eventuality of the end of our mortal sojourn here on earth. *Physical or mortal death* is as necessary a step in Father's plan for us as was our birth into this life. A separation of our spirit from our physical body at the time of our mortal death will happen to us all. Likewise, because each of us has sinned, we each face the certainty of being alienated from God's presence, which is called *spiritual death*.

The atoning sacrifice of the Son of God was foreordained by our Father to overcome for us the effects of both physical death and spiritual death. Except for the atoning sacrifice of the

Son of God and his resurrection from the dead, we would have forever remained subject to the effects of *physical death*, (that is, our spirit and our body of flesh and bones would forever remain separated after our physical death here on earth), and subject to *spiritual death*, the damning effects of our own personal sins which would forever prevent us from returning to the presence of God our Father. (See, 2 Nephi 2:15-27)

Jesus Christ was in the unique position to do for us what we could never do for ourselves. First, He was the son of a mortal woman, Mary, but he was also the son of the Great God of Heaven, an immortal exalted and glorified Man, in whose image and likeness we were created. As such, Jesus carried within him from his mortal mother the seeds of death. But from his immortal Father he carried the power over death. Christ said, as recorded in **John 10:17-18;**

**"Therefore doth my Father love me, because I lay down my life, that I might take it again. No man taketh it from me, but I lay it down of myself. I have power to lay it down, and I have power to take it again. This commandment have I received of my Father."** (John 10:17-18)

Second, Christ was the only man who has ever lived here on earth that perfectly followed Father's commandments, remaining sinless, while fulfilling Father's commandments to him. He was, in fact, "without blemish or spot." He was the only man who ever lived who was guiltless, and thereby worthy or capable of offering himself as the ultimate and infinite sacrifice to pay, with his own precious blood, the price for the sins of all mankind. Just how the atonement was accomplished, we cannot understand. Nor is it necessary for us to understand such.

Christ voluntarily submitted to the agony of the cross and the events that preceded the cross in the Garden of Gethsemane where he literally bled from every pore because the pain and suffering of his ordeal was so great. (Luke 22:44) He actually suffered the pain and agony (unimaginable to us) of the punishment for all of my sins, and yours. (D&C 19:16-19) Then, he voluntarily gave up his life on the cross. His spirit left his physical body and He voluntarily suffered a physical death. His body of flesh and bones was then hurriedly laid in a borrowed tomb on the eve of the Jewish Sabbath. And as the prophets had foretold, on the morning of the third day his spirit entered again into his body of flesh and bones, and he broke the bonds of physical death and rose from the grave, body and spirit inseparably reunited in eternal resurrected glory, never to die again.

The effects of this transcendent event are truly far reaching. Paul explained that while physical death came into the world by the actions of one man, meaning Adam, by one man, meaning Christ, physical death has been overcome for all men.

**"But now is Christ risen from the dead, and become the firstfruits of them that slept. For since by man came death, by man came also the resurrection of the dead. For as in Adam all die, even so in Christ shall all be made alive." (1 Corinthians 15:20-22)**

The great truth here taught is that "all" shall be made alive. Yes, this means exactly what is says. All men, good and bad, shall be resurrected. Their spirits and bodies shall be reunited, never to die again. Christ has overcome the effects of physical death brought into the world by Adam. Just as we, the posterity of Adam, had nothing to do with physical death coming into the world, we have nothing to do with it being overcome. Christ has given this great gift to all.

The prophets in the Americas taught this beautiful doctrine of the resurrection. The prophet Alma said:

**"The soul shall be restored to the body, and the body to the soul; yea, and every limb and joint shall be restored to its body; yea, even a hair of the head shall not be lost; but all things shall be restored to their proper and perfect frame." (Alma 40:23)**

After the resurrection of Christ, the gospel writer Matthew recorded:

**"...the graves were opened; and many bodies of the saints which slept arose, and came out of the graves after his resurrection, and went into the holy city, and appeared unto many." (Matthew 27:52-53)**

The effects of Adam's transgression which brought physical death into the world have been paid or overcome by Christ as a free gift to all men, and we will all be resurrected.

However, each of us must still deal with the consequences of our own personal sins. Christ clearly taught this as recorded in **John 5:28-29.**

**"Marvel not at this: for the hour is coming, in the which all that are in the graves shall hear his voice, and shall come forth; they that have done good, unto the resurrection of life; and they that have done evil, unto the resurrection of damnation."**

Christ broke the bonds of physical death for all of us. This means we will all be resurrected from the death of this body of flesh and bones that we are all so familiar with. However, we must all still deal with the effects of spiritual death. We must all then stand before the judgment bar of God to be judged according to our own deeds or works while here on earth. It will be then that those who have been washed clean of their own sins through the blood of the Lamb will be clean still, and they will be admitted back into the presence of the Father, while those who have not followed the teachings of the Savior and are found unclean then will remain unclean still, and they will forever be denied the glorious blessings of "Eternal Life" reserved for those who have overcome the world by keeping Christ's commandments and works "unto the end" of their life. (see, Revelation 2:26)

The Apostle John foresaw this great judgment at the last day and wrote of it with these words:

**"And I saw the dead, small and great, stand before God; and the books were opened: and another book was opened, which is the book of life: and the dead were judged out of those things which were written in the books, according to their works.**

**And the sea gave up the dead which were in it; and death and hell delivered up the dead which were in them: and they were judged every man according to their works." (Revelation 20:12-13)**

Yes, all of us must stand before the judgment bar of God and account for those things we have done, or not done, during our lives. We will be judged, every one of us, according to our "works," a doctrine that is contrary to the idea that we are saved by grace alone without regard for what we do. It is also contrary to the notion that "once saved, always saved" as championed by some churches of today.

As to the rewards or glories prepared for Father's children in the resurrection, we know that the ultimate reward is to merit returning to the presence of the Father and there to become "joint-heirs with Christ" (See, Romans 8:17), which means sharing all that the Father has (See, Romans 8:32; Revelation 21:7), and having a life like our Father and his Son Jesus Christ (See, Matthew 5:48; 1John 3:2), which the scriptures refer to as "Eternal Life" (John 10:28; 1 John 2:25). We also know that at the other end of the spectrum, those who have chosen to be followers of Satan will be cast into what is referred to as "outer darkness," a place of no glory that will be the ultimate dwelling of Satan and his followers. (See, Matthew 8: 12; Alma 40:13)

However, these extremes are not the only rewards prepared. Christ told his disciples;

**"In my Father's house are many mansions, if it were not so I would have told you." (John 14: 2)**

Paul taught in his letter to the Corinthians that there are three major degrees of glory in the resurrection, and referred to the highest as the "Celestial" and to the next as the "terrestrial," and likened their differences to the difference between the sun and the moon. But he also says there is another lower glory, which he likens to the stars:

**"There are also *celestial* bodies, and bodies *terrestrial*: but the glory of the celestial is one, and the glory of the terrestrial is another.**

**There is one glory of the sun, and another glory of the moon, and another glory of the stars: for one star differeth from another star in glory,**

So also is the resurrection of the dead. It is sown in corruption, it is raised in incorruption:" (1 Corinthians 15: 40-41)

As taught by Paul, there are three major degrees or kingdoms of glory in the resurrection: the celestial, the terrestrial, and revelation in these days has given us the name of the third, the telestial. Paul indicated that as one star differeth in glory from another, so also will be the resurrection of the dead.

Paul referred to the **"third heaven"** in his Second Epistle to the Corinthians.

"I knew a man in Christ above fourteen years ago, (whether in the body, I cannot tell; or whether out of the body, I cannot tell: God knoweth;) such an one caught up to the third heaven." (2 Corinthians 12:2)

In the resurrection we will receive the reward or glory that we deserve. However, it is only in the Celestial kingdom of glory where the Father and the Son dwell. To return to their presence and enjoy "eternal life" means to be worthy of the highest degree of the celestial glory. (See, D&C 76)

So, the question must then be asked:

**"WHAT MUST ONE DO TO BE WASHED CLEAN OF HIS OWN SINS THROUGH THE BLOOD OF CHRST?"**

Is believing in Christ all that is necessary? Is professing Christ and accepting him in our hearts all we need do? Or is there more that must be done?

Christ spoke of those who confess or accept Christ with their mouth, or give him lip service, but fail to keep his commandments.

"Not every one that saith unto me, Lord, Lord, shall enter into the kingdom of heaven; <u>but he that doeth the will of my Father</u> which is in heaven.

Many will say to me in that day Lord, Lord, have we not prophesied in thy name? and in thy name have cast out devils? And in thy name done many wonderful works?

And then will I profess unto them, I never knew you: depart from me, ye that work iniquity." (Matthew 7:21-23)

We see even then, as now, that "talk is cheap." It is the actual "doing" of our Father's will that is the important thing. In order to be "saved," or entitled to return to the presence of our Father and enjoy with Him a life like His, which we call "Eternal Life," one must **"do the will of my Father,"** or keep his commandments. The question then is, **"What exactly must we do to be washed clean of our sins?"**

This question is not left unanswered in the Holy Scriptures. This same question was posed to Peter and the other apostles during the feast of Pentecost by a group of sincere Jews who were gathered in Jerusalem in compliance with the Jewish law. With boldness, Peter had preached to these men, telling them that Jesus Christ was the Son of God, the Messiah, that he had been crucified by wicked men, and that he had risen from the dead. Peter bore a powerful witness to these men, and they believed his words and were pricked in their hearts. The book of Acts records the exchange between Peter and this group of men with these words:

**"Now when they heard this, they were pricked in their heart, and said unto Peter and to the rest of the apostles, _Men and brethren, what shall we do_?" (Acts 2: 37)**

These men clearly exhibited a degree of *faith*. They believed Peter's teachings and showed their desire to know what else they needed to do. They showed their willingness to take the next step, or to *do* something about their belief. When a person has learned of Jesus Christ, and believes him to be the Messiah or the Savior, and believes strongly enough to want to do something about his belief, this is FAITH. A correct or true demonstration of faith is a person who believes strongly enough to be willing to do something about his or her belief. Belief by itself alone is not faith. Belief coupled with a willingness to take action or to actually do something in furtherance of the belief is faith. These men speaking with Peter in Acts 2:37-38 showed their faith by demonstrating their desire to take the next step based on their belief in what Peter had taught them about the Savior.

The question asked by these men is the pertinent question that all believing men and women must ask themselves:

**"WHAT SHALL WE DO?"** Once a person feels the Holy Spirit in his heart and believes that Jesus Christ is the Son of God, and believes strongly enough to be willing to act on that belief, the next question naturally must be the same as posed by these men, ***WHAT MUST HE THEN DO?*** Peter answered the question very directly and simply.

"Then Peter said unto them, <u>Repent, and be baptized</u> every one of you <u>in the name of Jesus Christ for the remission of sins</u>, and ye shall <u>receive the gift of the Holy Ghost</u>." (Acts 2:38)

So, as taught by the Apostle Peter of old, the next steps to be taken by one after he believes in his heart and demonstrates his *faith* in the Lord Jesus Christ is to:

1. ***Repent*** of his sins:
2. ***Be baptized*** by immersion (as was Jesus) in the name of Jesus Christ by one having the authority to do so, for the remission of sins:
3. ***Receive the gift of the Holy Ghost*** by the laying on of hands by those having the authority to do so.

These steps are simple and clear: (1) Faith in the Lord Jesus Christ; (2) Repentance of one's own personal sins; (3) Baptism by immersion in the name of Jesus Christ, by one having Christ's authority to do so, for the remission of sins; and (4) Receiving the Gift of the Holy Ghost by the laying on of hands by those who have Christ's authority to do so.

There are many Christian churches in the world today who believe that baptism is optional in spite of the teachings of Peter from the Bible. They believe that baptism is not necessary in order to be washed clean of our sins, or necessary to return to the presence of God, or to enter into the kingdom of God. It would, therefore, be appropriate to point out what the Savior himself said about the importance of baptism in his conversation with Nicodemus, who came to Christ by night to obviously ask the Savior about what must he do to enter into the kingdom of God. The Savior's reply is very instructive:

"Jesus answered and said unto him, Verily, verily, I say unto thee, Except a man be born again, he cannot see the kingdom of God.

Nicodemus saith unto him, How can a man be born when he is old? Can he enter the second time into his mother's womb, and be born?

Jesus answered, Verily, verily, I say unto thee, <u>Except a man be born of water and of the Spirit, he cannot enter into the kingdom of God.</u>" (John 3: 3-5)

To be **"born of water"** is baptism. To be born **"of the Spirit"** is the receipt of the gift of the Holy Ghost by the laying on of hands, as was uniformly practiced in the early church. Christ says very clearly that except a man is baptized, i.e., born of the water, and receives the gift of the Holy Ghost by the laying on of hands, i.e., born of the Spirit, he cannot enter into the kingdom of God.

Immediately before Christ's ascension into heaven from the slopes of the Mount of Olives just east of the City of Jerusalem, Christ gave some final instructions to his apostles. What is undoubtedly a brief summary of those instructions is recorded in the book of Mark, where we find this simple statement by the Savior about the critical importance of baptism.

"He that believeth and is baptized shall be saved; but he that believeth not shall be damned." (Mark 16:16)

No more authoritative statements can exist than from the mouth of the Savior himself, and from his apostles. One would ignore the requirement of baptism to his own everlasting detriment!

A prophet in the America's taught these same beautiful truths about baptism.

"And now, if the Lamb of God, he being holy, should have need to be baptized by water, to fulfill all righteousness, O then, how much more need have we, being unholy, to be baptized, yea, even by water!

And now, I would ask of you, my beloved brethren, wherein the Lamb of God did fulfill all righteousness in being baptized by water?

"Know ye not that he was holy? But notwithstanding he being holy, he showeth unto the children of men that, according to the flesh he humbleth himself before the Father, and witnesseth unto the Father that he would be obedient unto him in keeping his commandments.

Wherefore, after he was baptized with water the Holy Ghost descended upon him in the form of a dove.

And again, it showeth unto the children of men the straitness of the path, and the narrowness of the gate, by which they should enter, he having set the example before them.

And he said unto the children of men: Follow thou me. Wherefore, my beloved brethren, can we follow Jesus save we shall be willing to keep the commandments of the Father?" **(2 Nephi 31: 5- 10)**

There is no question that baptism by immersion for the remission of sins by one having the priesthood of God, and then receiving the gift of the Holy Ghost by the laying on of hands, again by one having the priesthood authority to do so, are requirements set by our Savior to enter into the kingdom of God. The steps that make up the strait and narrow way through which all must pass to enter in at the gate into the kingdom of God are clear and concise, and are set out in the Holy Scriptures without any confusion for he who will study and listen to the Savior's words. The Savior's way is the only way.

(I will address in ESSAY SEVEN: THE PRIESTHOOD OF GOD, pg 66, the topic of the necessity of **priesthood authority** to perform a valid baptism and other priesthood ordinances such as the laying on of hands for the gift of the Holy Ghost. Suffice it to say at this point that in the early church and in the days of the early apostles, the authority given by Christ to his apostles, or the priesthood, was clearly necessary in order to perform valid ordinances including baptism and the laying on of hands for the Gift of the Holy Ghost.)

Once one accomplishes these steps of faith, repentance, baptism, and receiving the Gift of the Holy Ghost, is all then done? Once we have been washed clean of our sins in the waters of baptism, are we then "saved," or home free, so to speak? No, the Bible makes it abundantly clear that we must *keep Christ's works or commandments to the end of our life.* (Revelation 2: 26)

A prophet in the Americas addressed this same question with this prophetic counsel:

"**And now, my beloved brethren, I know by this that unless a man shall endure to the end, in following the example of the Son of the living God, he cannot be saved.**

**Wherefore, do the things which I have told you I have seen that your Lord and your Redeemer should do; for, for this cause have they been shown unto me, that ye might know the gate by which ye should enter. For the gate by which ye should enter is repentance and baptism by water; and then cometh a remission of your sins by fire and by the Holy Ghost.**

**And then are ye in this strait and narrow path which leads to eternal life; yea, ye have entered in by the gate; ye have done according to the commandments of the Father and the Son; and ye have received the Holy Ghost, which witnesses of the Father and the Son, unto the fulfilling of the promise which he hath made, that if ye entered in by the way ye should receive.**

**And now, my beloved brethren, after ye have gotten into this strait and narrow path, I would ask if all is done? Behold, I say unto you, Nay; for ye have not come thus far save it were by the word of Christ with unshaken faith in him, relying wholly upon the merits of him who is mighty to save.**

**Wherefore, ye must press forward with a steadfastness of hope, and a love of God and of all men. Wherefore, if ye shall press forward, feasting upon the word of Christ, and endure to the end, behold, thus saith the Father: Ye shall have eternal life.**

**And now, behold, my beloved brethren, this is the way; and there is none other way nor name given under heaven whereby man can be saved in the kingdom of God. And now, behold, this is the doctrine of Christ, and the only**

**and true doctrine of the Father, and of the Son, and of the Holy Ghost, which is one God, without end. Amen." (2 Nephi 31: 16-21)**

Our Heavenly Father's plan for us, his children, is to allow us as his offspring the opportunity to progress from being his spirit children who lived with him in the heavens prior to the creation of this world, to become perfected like our Father by coming to this earth to gain a physical body, to be tried and tested, to develop and prove our own faith and our obedience to his commandments in the face of trials and opposition; and if we are faithful in obeying and following his commandments to the end of our lives we may return to his presence to enjoy with our Father and our Eldest Brother, the Son of God, our Savior and Redeemer, Jesus Christ, the blessings of Eternal Life.

Central to this plan was and is the atoning sacrifice of our Savior Jesus Christ. We know that without the atonement and saving grace of the Son of God, our Savior Jesus Christ, we would have no hope of being able to return to the presence of our Father. But we also know that it is only if we are willing to live our lives in accordance with his teachings and the principles he has taught us and continues to teach us through his servants the prophets that we may achieve the realization of that "hope of eternal life" promised to us by our Father before the world began. (Titus 1:2) The prophet Nephi in ancient America wrote these words:

**"For we labor diligently to write, to persuade our children, and also our brethren, to believe in Christ, and to be reconciled to God; for we know that it is by grace that we are saved, after all we can do." (2 Nephi 25: 23)**

We know and understand these truths, not because we read the Bible better than our Protestant friends. We know them because God has again restored these eternal gospel truths to the earth through living prophets of God, called by God in these last days to once again restore to his children on earth the precious truths of His plan for us, his children, which have been taught by Him through His holy prophets since the beginning of the world.

I bear my personal witness that these things are true.

59

## *Essay Six*

## "THE OFFSPRING OF GOD"

The question is often posed by our Protestant friends, "Do you Mormons really believe you can become gods?" For those who are honestly interested in learning what we in fact believe, rather than what their own pastor has told them, I explain to them that what we actually believe about man's relationship to God, and about man's Divine potential is exactly what is taught in the Bible. Then I take them through this series of scriptures.

In Genesis we learn that we were created in God's own image.

"And God said, <u>Let us make man in our image, after our likeness</u>;…So God created man in his own image, in the image of God created he him; male and female created he them." (Genesis 1:26-27)

Paul taught that we are literally the "offspring" of God. In his words to the Athenians at Mars Hill Paul taught the Greeks that God is not like one of their stone statutes.

"For in him we live, and move, and have our being; as certain also of your own poets have said. For <u>we are also his offspring</u>. Forasmuch then as we are the <u>offspring of God</u>, we ought not to think that the Godhead is like unto gold, or silver, or stone, graven by art and man's device." (Acts 17: 28-29)

In his epistle to the Romans, Paul further taught that we are the children of God.

"The Spirit itself beareth witness with our spirit, that <u>we are the children of God:</u>" (Romans 8: 16)

What is more natural than that the offspring of something should grow up to become like its parent. Christ, in fact, commanded us in his Sermon on the Mount that we should grow up and become like our Father. In **Mathew 5:48**, as the culminating commandment of the great "Sermon on the Mount," Christ commanded, **"<u>Be ye therefore *perfect*, even as your Father which is in heaven is *perfect.*</u>"** (Matthew 5:48)

What does it mean to be "*perfect*"? The Greek word from which the word "perfect" in our King James translation of the Bible is translated means "complete, finished, fully developed." Christ was commanding us to become "complete, finished, fully developed" like our Father in heaven.

Paul also taught that as the children of God, we are His *heirs*, and that we may become joint heirs with Christ, if we are willing to be obedient to his commandments. In **Romans 8:17** Paul concludes his statement that we are the children of God by saying:

"**And if children, then heirs; Heirs of God, and joint heirs with Christ; if so be that we suffer with him, that we may be also glorified together.**" (**Romans 8:17**)

Paul teaches here that we may become joint heirs with Christ if we are willing to suffer with Christ by keeping his commandments and being obedient to his teachings, so that we may be glorified together.

What does it mean to be a "**joint heir with Christ**"? The natural meaning of "joint heirs" as used in a last will and testament would be for various individuals to each inherit joint ownership of the same asset or estate.

John the Revelator explains exactly what it means to be a Joint heir with Christ. In his book of Revelation, John repeatedly speaks of the person who "**overcometh.**" To "overcome" is explained in **Revelation 2:26**.

"**And he that overcometh, and keepeth my works unto the end...**"

To "**overcome**" means to *overcome the world by keeping Christ's commandments to the end of our life.* With that explanation, John quotes the words of our Lord to him.

"**To him that overcometh will I grant to sit with me in my throne, even as I also overcame, and am set down with my Father in his throne.**" (Revelation 3:21)

The symbolism here is very clear. The Great King, our Father, has invited Christ, his son and rightful heir, who has "overcome," to sit beside him in his throne, symbolizing the Great King's recognition of his Son as sharing with him all that the Great King has, without limit, that is, his power and glory and his kingdoms and possessions. Even the Great King's own purposes and works are shared by the Son. They figuratively become "one." Christ then tells us that if we are willing to "overcome," or in other words keep his works or commandments to the end of our life, then he, Christ, will slide over and invite us to also come sit beside him in his Father's throne, which has now become his throne. This represents, symbolically, the recognition by Christ of those who have "overcome," as his father recognized him, meaning that he will share with all those who have "overcome" his inheritance from the Father in the same way the Father has shared all with him. Hence, they become "joint heirs" with Christ.

Christ and our Father promise those who are willing to "overcome" that they will share with them all they have, meaning their power and glory, and their kingdoms and possessions. Even the purposes and works of the Father and his Son become theirs also. In this way, those who have "overcome" will also become "one" with the Father and the Son, as was Christ's great Intercessory Prayer to the Father found in **John 17: 20-24.**

**"Neither pray I for these alone, but for them also which shall believe on me through their word; <u>That they all may be one; as thou, Father, art in me, and I in thee, that they also may be one in us</u>: that the world may believe that thou hast sent me. And the glory which thou gavest me I have given them; <u>that they may be one, even as we are one: I in them, and thou in me, that they may be *made perfect* in one;…</u>"**

In this way, those who "overcome" will have literally become **"perfect"** like their Father in heaven as Christ commanded in **Matthew 5:48.**

That this is the correct interpretation of the meaning of these scriptures, that Christ and the Father have promised to share all they have with those who are willing to be obedient to the end of their life in keeping their commandments, there is no doubt. John, again, in **Revelation 21:7,** assures us in the words of our Lord:

"He that overcometh shall inherit all things; and I will be his God, and he shall be my son." (Revelation 21:7)

Paul likewise teaches this very same thing in **Romans 8:32:**

"He [*meaning, the Father*] **that spared not his own Son, but delivered him up for us all, how shall he** [*meaning, the Father*] **not with him** [*meaning, the Son*] **also freely give us all things.**"

This same doctrine was restored through the Lord's prophet in these last days. The Lord's revelation to Joseph Smith recorded in Doctrine and Covenants Section 84, known as the "Oath and Covenant of the Priesthood" says:

"**For whoso is faithful unto the obtaining these two priesthoods of which I have spoken, and the magnifying their calling, are sanctified by the Spirit unto the renewing of their bodies.**

"**They become the sons of Moses and of Aaron and the seed of Abraham, and the church and kingdom, and the elect of God.**

"**And also all they who receive this priesthood receive me, saith the Lord;**

"**For he that receiveth my servants receiveth me;**

"**And he that receiveth me receiveth my Father;**

"**And <u>he that receiveth my Father receiveth my Father's kingdom; therefore all that my Father hath shall be given unto him.</u>** (D&C 84:33-39)

A vision given to the Prophet Joseph Smith and his associate Sidney Rigdon in 1832 showed them the Celestial glory, where God, the Father, and his Son, Jesus Christ, dwell. Though the Joint Heirs with Christ will share equally through Christ all of the Father's glories, dominions, and powers, as well as his works and purposes, all will forever bow in humble reverence and obedience before the God and Father of us all.

"And thus we saw the glory of the celestial, which excels in all things—where God, even the Father, reigns upon his throne forever and ever;

Before whose throne all things bow in humble reverence, and give him glory forever and ever.

They who dwell in his presence are the church of the Firstborn; and they see as they are seen, and know as they are known, having received of his fulness and of his grace;

And he makes them equal in power, and in might, and in dominion." (Doctrine and Covenants 76: 92-95)

Clearly, God's plan for his children, as taught from before the foundations of the world were laid, is to provide the opportunity,... that is the "hope,"... but not the guarantee,... of us returning to our Father's presence, and there to become perfected like our Father in heaven, and share with our Father and his Son, Jesus Christ, all things. This ultimate of blessings or rewards has been referred to often in the scriptures as **"eternal life,"** and it has been the goal for us from the beginning. In the book of Titus, in the New Testament, Paul taught that Father promised us the **"hope of eternal life"** even before the world was created.

"Paul, a servant of God, and an apostle of Jesus Christ, according to the faith of God's elect, and the acknowledging of the truth which is after godliness:

"In <u>hope of eternal life</u>, which <u>God, that cannot lie, promised before the world began</u>:" (Titus 1:1-2)

This is Father's plan for his children. Our Savior has said:

"This is my work and my glory to bring to pass the *immortality* and *eternal life* of man." (Moses 1:39)

"*Immortality*," meaning to live forever as resurrected beings which is a free gift to us all from our Lord and Savior; "*Eternal Life*," which is the reward prepared for and promised to all those who overcome the world by keeping the works or commandments of our Lord to the end of their life, which entitles them to return to the presence of our Father and his Son Jesus Christ, and there enjoy a life like our Father, sharing with the Father and his Son all that they have.

Christ was selected from before the foundations of the world were laid to be the ultimate sacrifice, as the lamb without blemish, to wash us clean from our sins through his own precious blood.

"But **with the precious blood of Christ, as of a lamb without blemish and without spot:** Who verily **was foreordained before the foundation of the world**, but was manifest in these last times for you." **(1 Peter 1:19-20)**

It is only through the atoning sacrifice of our Lord Jesus Christ that the way is provided for us to be able to be washed clean from our sins so that we may return to the presence of our Father and there become "perfect," like Him, "one" with our Father and his Son, Jesus Christ, "joint heirs with Christ," sharing "all things", which is "eternal life."

The mission and atoning sacrifice of our Lord and Savior Jesus Christ, the only begotten of the Father in the flesh, was from the beginning, and continues to be, the very heart of our Father's plan for the exaltation of his children.

John, called the *"Beloved"* and the *"Revelator,"* recorded these words of Christ as he prepared his disciples for his departure, that **"the Holy Ghost…shall teach you all things" (John 14:26)** and that **"he will guide you into all truth:" (John 16:13).** As you read and allow these precious truths to permeate your soul, listen to the whisperings of the Holy Spirit spoken of by our Lord. And if your heart is open, you will hear and feel that these precious teachings are true.

Of this, my sweet children, I testify.

*Essay Seven*

## THE PRIESTHOOD OF GOD

A topic that has been completely ignored by Christian sects in the world today is the Doctrine of Priesthood Authority. Why? Simply because the Christian sects of the world today don't have any authority, other than that which can be bestowed by man; nor do they pretend to have such. They are completely absent on the subject. Consequently, they simply avoid the topic.

At the beginning of Christ's ministry, he called twelve of his disciples and he *"ordained"* them to be Apostles, and gave to them his *"power"* and his *"authority"* to preach the gospel, heal the sick, cast out devils, baptize, and to generally perform acts or ordinances in the name of Jesus Christ and on his behalf here on the earth.

Mark observed:

"...and he *ordained* twelve, that they should be with him, and that he might send them forth to preach, and *to have power* to heal sicknesses, and to cast out devils;" (Mark 3:13-15)

Luke wrote:

"Then he called his twelve disciples together, and gave them *power and authority* over all devils, and to cure diseases. And he sent them to preach the kingdom of God, and to heal the sick." (Luke 9:1-2)

John recorded the words of Christ concerning this subject as:

"Ye have not chosen me, but *I have chosen you*, and *ordained* you, that ye should go and bring forth fruit,..." (John 15:16)

Later in his ministry Christ gave to his apostles the "**keys of the kingdom of heaven**". These were the keys to administer in the matters of the Kingdom of heaven on earth and the sealing power of the priesthood given to the apostles to bind or seal things on earth and in heaven. It is with this sealing authority that the work of sealing husbands and wives and their families together for the eternities was then, and is now accomplished.

**"And I will give unto thee the keys of the kingdom of heaven: and whatsoever thou shalt bind on earth shall be bound in heaven: and whatsoever thou shalt loose on earth shall be loosed in heaven."** (Matthew 16: 19)

These "keys of the kingdom" obviously represented a very special authority or power given to the apostles to bind or seal on earth and in heaven. How could one say that "authority" was not a key factor in the operation of the early church as it was set up by Christ?

Jesus also called other **"Seventy"** and gave them his **"power" (Luke 10: 1-2, 19)** and sent them out two by two before him into the cities of Judea to preach his gospel and to prepare the way before him.

It is clear that this practice of "ordaining" those who were called to perform priesthood callings, to give them the power and authority to perform their calling, was followed by the early church. In the period after the ascension of Christ into heaven, the Apostles selected seven men with the specific calling to minister to the widows of the Church around Jerusalem;

**"whom they set before the apostles: and when they had prayed, they laid their hands on them."** (Acts 6: 6)

This is the classic method of "ordaining" someone to a priesthood calling; That is, for the Priesthood holder that has the authority to lay his hands upon the person who is being called and to ordain or confer upon the person being called the power and authority to fulfill his calling.

In Paul's letter to Titus, Paul instructed Titus who had been called and ordained by Paul to be a Bishop in the early Church at Crete, to **"set in order the things that are wanting, and _ordain_ elders in every city, as I had appointed thee:" (Titus 1:5)** Priesthood authority was clearly necessary in the administration of the early church.

In Paul's letter to the Hebrews, he taught extensively about the priesthood. In Chapter 5 of Hebrews Paul teaches:

"For every high priest taken from among men is *ordained* for men in things pertaining to God,..." (Hebrews 5: 1)

Paul then goes on to explain that:

"**no man taketh this honour unto himself, but he that is called of God, as was Aaron.**" (Hebrews 1: 4)

No man can call himself to the priesthood. He must be called by God as was Aaron, the brother of Moses. And how was Aaron called? The Lord told Moses to call Aaron, and Moses laid his hands on Aaron and ordained him, he gave him the authority or power of the priesthood to function in his office. (Exodus 4:14-16)

In the Book of Hebrews, Paul teaches that there are two priesthoods. One is called the priesthood *after the order of Melchisedec.* Paul describes Christ as a "**High Priest forever after the order of Melchisedec.**" (Hebrews 5: 6, 10) The other priesthood he refers to as the *Levitical priesthood*, or the priesthood *after the order of Aaron.* (Hebrews 7: 11) Paul indicates that the Melchisedec Priesthood is the higher priesthood, held by Christ himself and given to his apostles.

The Levitical Priesthood is the lesser priesthood held by the men of the tribe of Levi, who received this priesthood by lineage from their fathers. Aaron, the brother of Moses, was of the tribe of Levi and he and his sons or lineal descendants after him were designated by Moses to be the high priests of the Levitical priesthood or order, which has been known since then as the priesthood after the order of Aaron, or the Aaronic Priesthood. This was the lesser priesthood that helped or officiated in the sacrificial offerings at the temple under the Mosaic law. The descendants of Aaron officiated in the temple as high priests, and were assisted with the sacrifices by the Levites. The lineal descendants of Aaron officiated in the temple, and possessed the priesthood after the order of Aaron by right of birth. (For a more extensive discussion of these two priesthoods, the Melchisedec and the Aaronic or Levitical, see D&C Section 107.)

John the Baptist was the son of Zacharias, who was a lineal descendant of Aaron. Zacharias, as a high priest after the Aaronic Priesthood, was officiating in the Holy of Holies in the Temple at Jerusalem when the angel of the Lord appeared to him announcing the birth of his son to be called John. (Luke 1: 5-23) John, as a lineal descendant of Aaron, possessed the Aaronic Priesthood by right of birth, and as such was a legal administrator in the kingdom and could perform valid baptisms with this priesthood, but could not give the gift of the Holy Ghost. To bestow the gift of the Holy Ghost by the laying on of hands requires the Melchisedec, or higher priesthood.

When John the Baptist embarked on his mission of baptizing and announcing the coming of the Christ, Matthew records:

"**Then went out to him Jerusalem and all Judaea, and all the region round about Jordan, and were baptized of him in Jordan, confessing their sins.**" (Matthew 3:5)

In his ministry, John announced to the people:

"**I indeed baptize you with water unto repentance: but he that cometh after me is mightier than I, whose shoes I am not worthy to bear: he shall baptize you with the Holy Ghost, and with fire:**" (Matthew 3: 11)

So, Christ was baptized by John, the son of Zacharias, a legal administrator in the kingdom of God who clearly possessed the Aaronic Priesthood with the authority to baptize.

In evaluating the issue of priesthood authority with respect to the early Church, one must address the question, "Was the proper priesthood authority necessary to perform a valid baptism in the early Church?" The short answer is "Yes, absolutely."

There are two incidents reported in the Book of Acts that teach very clearly the necessity of the proper priesthood to both baptize and to perform the laying on of hands to give the Gift of the Holy Ghost after baptism. The first is in **Acts 8: 9-20;**

"**But there was a certain man, called Simon, which beforetime in the same city used sorcery, and bewitched the** people of Samaria, giving out that himself was some great one:

To whom they all gave heed, from the least to the greatest, saying, This man is the great power of God.

And to him they had regard, because that of long time he had bewitched them with sorceries.

But when they believed Philip preaching the things concerning the kingdom of God, and the name of Jesus Christ, they were baptized, both men and women.

Then Simon himself believed also: and when he was baptized, he continued with Philip, and wondered, beholding the miracles and signs which were done.

Now when the apostles which were at Jerusalem heard that Samaria had received the word of God, they sent unto them Peter and John:

Who, when they were come down, prayed for them, that they might receive the Holy Ghost:

(For as yet he was fallen upon none of them: only they were baptized in the name of the Lord Jesus.)

Then laid they *their* hands on them, and they received the Holy Ghost.

And when Simon saw that through laying on of the apostles' hands the Holy Ghost was given, he offered them money,

Saying, Give me also this power, that on whomsoever I lay hands, he may receive the Holy Ghost.

"But Peter said unto him, Thy money perish with thee, because thou hast thought that the gift of God may be purchased with money." **(Acts 8: 9-20)**

Phillip, who certainly held the Aaronic priesthood and could perform valid baptisms, was teaching in Samaria and baptized a number of converts. However, since he didn't hold the higher priesthood after the order of Melchisedec he did not have the authority to lay hands on the converts to give them the gift of the Holy Ghost. When the apostles in Jerusalem heard of the converts they sent Peter and John, two apostles, who when they had come, **"laid they their hands on them, and they**

**received the Holy Ghost."** Clearly, priesthood authority was requisite to perform the ordinances of baptism and of the laying on of hands for the gift of the Holy Ghost.

It is also interesting to note here that Simon, who had previously been a sorcerer but who had been baptized by Phillip, sought to pay money to Peter in an attempt to purchase from him this priesthood authority to enable him to give the Gift of the Holy Ghost by the laying on of hands. Peter told Simon that his money would perish with him, because he thought to purchase the gift of God (the priesthood authority) with money. It couldn't be purchased with money anciently, and neither can it be purchased with money today.

In Chapter 19 of Acts, verses 1-6, another pertinent incident is recorded. As Paul was passing through the coasts near Ephesus, he came upon certain disciples who professed to be members of the church. Paul obviously did not know these disciples, and asked them, **"Have ye received the Holy Ghost since ye believed?"** Their response was: **"We have not so much as heard whether there be any Holy Ghost."** This surprised Paul because if these were true converts, baptized by one of his brethren with the priesthood who were traveling and preaching the gospel, they would surely have been taught about the laying on of hands to receive the Gift of the Holy Ghost. Paul's next question was, **"Unto what then were ye baptized?"** It's interesting here that Paul doesn't ask, "Who baptized you?", but rather he asks, "Unto *what* were you baptized?" They obviously were not baptized by any of Paul's brethren with the priesthood of God because they would have been taught about the gift of the Holy Ghost. Their response was, **"Unto John's baptism."** Paul immediately knew that certainly John didn't baptize these people because John would have taught them about the coming Christ who would baptize with fire and with the Holy Ghost. Paul said;

**"John verily baptized with the baptism of repentance, saying believe on him which should come after him, that is, on Christ Jesus."** (Acts 19: 4)

The story concludes with these converts being re-baptized by one having the proper priesthood authority.

"**When they heard this, they were baptized in the name of the Lord Jesus. And when Paul had laid his hands upon them, the Holy Ghost came on them; and they spake with tongues, and prophesied.**" (Acts 19: 5-6)

This is a case where well intentioned people had in fact been baptized but by someone who did not have the priesthood authority to do so. If any baptism were acceptable, Paul would have simply welcomed them into the flock and proceeded with giving them the Gift of the Holy Ghost. But such was not the case. He taught them correct doctrine and they were then baptized over again by one having the proper priesthood authority to do so. They were then given the Gift of the Holy Ghost by the laying on of hands by Paul himself who had the higher priesthood after the order of Melchisedec.

In the days of the early church, as it is today, good intentions are not a substitute for proper priesthood authority in performing the ordinances, such as baptism, in the kingdom of God.

In the same chapter 19 of Acts, verses 13-16, there is another incident that emphasizes the critical nature of having the proper priesthood authority in performing priesthood ordinances. There were several young Jews who were in fact the sons of one of the local magistrates. These young men took it upon themselves to try to cast out an evil spirit that had possessed a certain man. They did so by using "**the name of the Lord Jesus, saying, We adjure you by Jesus whom Paul preacheth.**" (ibid., verse 13)

It is interesting to note the reaction of the evil spirit to the young imposters who were acting as if they had authority to act in the name of Jesus.

"**... And the evil spirit answered and said, Jesus I know, and Paul I know; but who are ye? And the man in whom the evil spirit was leaped on them, and overcame them, and prevailed against them, so that they fled out of that house naked and wounded.**" (ibid., verse 16)

Can there be any doubt that proper priesthood authority was necessary in the early church of Jesus Christ to perform a valid baptism or any other priesthood ordinance? Can there be any doubt that proper priesthood authority would be necessary to effectuate a valid baptism or any other priesthood ordinance in the true Church of Jesus Christ when ever it may exist?

If the true church of Jesus Christ has been restored to the earth, would you not expect the true priesthood authority to be restored with it? On May 15, 1829, the young Prophet Joseph Smith and his scribe Oliver Cowdrey were engaged in the translation of the plates entrusted to him by the angel Moroni, as instructed by the angel. In the course of the translation, reference had been made to baptism, and Joseph and Oliver were anxious to know more concerning baptism for the remission of sins. So they determined to pray and to ask God for more light and knowledge on the subject. After retiring to a private area of woods, they knelt and prayed. The words of Joseph relate what happened in the course of their prayer.

**"A messenger from heaven descended in a cloud of light, and having laid his hands upon us, he ordained us, saying:** *Upon you my fellow servants, in the name of Messiah, I confer the Priesthood of Aaron, which holds the keys of the ministering of angels and of the gospel of repentance, and of baptism by immersion for the remission of sins; and this shall never be taken again from the earth until the sons of Levi do offer again an offering unto the Lord in righteousness.* **He said this Aaronic Priesthood had not the power of laying on hands for the gift of the Holy Ghost, but that this should be conferred on us hereafter; and he commanded us to go and be baptized, and gave us directions that I should baptize Oliver Cowdrey, and that afterwards he should baptize me." (Joseph Smith History 1: 68-69)**

The messenger who visited Joseph and Oliver on this occasion said that his name was John, the same as was called John the Baptist in the New Testament, and that he acted under the direction of Peter, James and John, who held the keys of the priesthood of Melchizedek, which, he said, would, in due time, be conferred upon them.

Approximately one month after that glorious event, under similar surroundings, the three ancient apostles, Peter, James and John, appeared in a glorious manifestation to the young prophet Joseph, and to his companion Oliver Cowdrey, and conferred upon them the keys of the Melchizedek Priesthood, the authority given them by the Savior himself while they were on the earth.

The priesthood of God has been restored to the earth. In the restored church today, those who hold the Melchizedek priesthood can trace the lineage of the priesthood they have received directly to Peter, James, and John, who restored the priesthood in this day, and then to the Master himself. With that priesthood, we on earth again have the opportunity to have the fullness of the blessings of the gospel of Jesus Christ in our lives. The true Church of Jesus Christ has been organized again on the earth under the direction of the Savior himself, who has called prophets of God in these days to bring about that **"restitution of all things which God hath spoken by the mouth of all his holy prophets since the world began." (Acts 3:21)**

If one is not really concerned with finding the true church of Jesus Christ, then any baptism will do. However, if one is concerned with being baptized by one having the proper priesthood authority so as to effectuate a valid and efficacious baptism that will wash him clean from his sins and allow him entrance into the kingdom of God, then finding the true church of Jesus Christ is critical because it is only in the true church in which one will find the true priesthood of God.

Of these things I bear to you my witness that they are true.

*Essay Eight*

## SALVATION FOR THE LIVING AND THE DEAD

We know from truths revealed by God to his prophets here on earth that we are the offspring or children of God (Acts 17:28-29; Romans 8:16)); that we lived with him in the heavens as his children before the foundations of the earth were laid (Jeremiah 1:5; Ephesians 1:4-5); that we are the beneficiaries of a glorious plan of our Father in heaven (Titus 1:2) to provide an opportunity for us, his children, to progress from the spirits we were in our premortal or first estate with the plan, even the commandment, for us to become "perfect" like our Father (Matthew 5:48).

We know that this plan, of which we are now participants, included the preparation of this earth to which we could come to gain a physical body as mortals, to be tried and tested in all things, to develop our own faith, and to see if we are willing to be obedient to our Father's commandments while here on earth in the face of temptation and opposition (Abraham 3:22-28).

We know that the central theme of Father's plan was the role assigned to Father's Firstborn spirit offspring, his Son, Jesus Christ, to be our Savior and Messiah. We know that Christ was foreordained while still a spirit before the world was created to come to earth at the appointed time to be the long awaited "lamb without blemish and without spot" who would, with his own precious blood, atone for the sins of the world, of all mankind. (1 Peter 1:19-20).

The great relevance of this atoning sacrifice is that it overcomes for us the effects of physical death (1 Corinthians 15:20-22; Alma 11;42-45), and affords each of us the great blessing of being washed clean of our own sins so as to be worthy of entering again into the presence of our Father (Alma 42).

We've also learned that Christ has established a narrow path for us to follow in order for us to be washed clean of our own personal sins, which includes; (1) Faith in the Lord Jesus

Christ; (2) Repentance by us of our own personal sins; (3) Baptism by immersion in the name of Jesus Christ, by one having his authority or priesthood, for the remission of sins; (4) receiving the Gift of the Holy Ghost by the laying on of hands by one having Christ's authority or priesthood (See, Acts 2:37-38); and (5) persevere or keep his works or commandments to the end of our life (Revelation 2:26; 2 Nephi 31:16-21).

If these steps are necessary for a person to be washed clean of his sins, (and we know that they are necessary) what about the majority of people who have lived on earth and died without ever hearing of Jesus Christ while in this life, much less having an opportunity to actually understand the truth about God and his plan for us? Are they simply lost or damned as most of modern Christianity supposes? Or has our Father prepared a way, as part of his great plan, for those who die in ignorance to be given an opportunity to hear and learn of Christ, and participate in his saving ordinances? And if so, where is such taught?

The short answer is "yes," Father has provided a way as part of his great plan for those who died without an opportunity to hear and learn of and accept the gospel of Jesus Christ while here on earth to be provided such an opportunity. Would you expect our Father, God, to have a plan so inherently unfair and flawed so as to damn the great majority of his children to failure in their mortal trial without ever giving them a chance? Hardly!

Where is it taught? In the Holy Bible. Follow me through this chronology. When Christ finished his great work on the cross he "gave up the ghost" and his spirit left his body of flesh and bones and his physical body suffered mortal death. His spirit, however, certainly did not die. His physical body was placed in the tomb. On the morning of the third day his spirit returned to reunite with his body of flesh and bones in resurrected glory, never to be separated again, never to die again.

The reality of the resurrection is indisputable. On the morning of the resurrection, one of the first persons to see the risen Savior was Mary Magdalene who had come to the garden tomb early in the morning to finish the work of preparation of the

Savior's body that had been so hastily begun on Friday afternoon as the body of Christ was taken down from the cross and laid in the tomb. The point of interest I wish to make is that as Mary recognized the Master, she attempted to embrace him, and Christ restrained her with these words:

"...Touch me not; *for I am not yet ascended to my Father*: but go to my brethren, and say unto them, I ascend unto my Father, and your Father; and to my God, and your God." (John 20:17)

The question becomes obvious, if Christ's spirit had not yet gone to his Father in heaven during the period of time while his physical body was in the tomb separated from his spirit, where indeed had it gone? While on the cross, Christ told one of the thieves who was crucified along side him, **"today thou shalt be with me in paradise."** (Luke 23:43) Most assume that Christ was telling the thief that he would be in heaven with the Savior on that day. But we learn from the mouth of Christ that his spirit did not go to his Father in heaven during the period of separation from his physical body. So then where did it go?

Peter tells us in his first epistle.

**"For Christ also hath once suffered for sins, the just for the unjust, that he might bring us to God, being put to death in the flesh, but quickened by the Spirit: *By which also he went and preached unto the spirits in prison*; which sometime were disobedient, when once the longsuffering of God waited in the days of Noah, while the ark was a preparing, wherein few, that is, eight souls were saved by water."** (1 Peter 3:18-20)

We learn here that Christ's spirit went to the place where disembodied spirits await the day of their resurrection and preached the gospel to the disobedient spirits there who were in "prison;" "Prison," meaning spirits who were in bondage to ignorance and sin. So, when Christ told the thief on the cross that he would be with him that day in "paradise," he in fact meant the world where all disembodied spirits go to await the day of their resurrection. For some, the repentant and the righteous, their wait in the world of spirits will be a rest of peace, as a paradise.

For others who are in bondage to sin and ignorance, their wait is obviously like a prison.

The Book of Mormon Prophet Alma taught these enlightening truths about the period between our mortal death and the reuniting of our physical body and our spirit in the resurrection.

"Now, concerning the state of the soul between death and the resurrection...

And then shall it come to pass, that the spirits of those who are righteous are received into a state of happiness, which is called paradise, a state of rest, a state of peace, where they shall rest from all their troubles and from all care, and sorrow.

And then shall it come to pass, that the spirits of the wicked, yea, who are evil—for behold, they have no part nor portion of the Spirit of the Lord; for behold, they chose evil works rather than good; therefore the spirit of the devil did enter into them, and take possession of their house—and these shall be cast out into outer darkness; there shall be weeping, and wailing, and gnashing of teeth, and this because of their own iniquity, being led captive by the will of the devil. Now this is the state of the souls of the wicked, yea, in darkness, and a state of awful, fearful looking for the fiery indignation of the wrath of God upon them; thus they remain in this state, as well as the righteous in paradise, until the time of their resurrection." (Alma 40: 11-14)

Peter continued in his epistle to explain why the gospel was preached to the spirits of the dead (although the reason is obvious). Those who have died in mortality without learning of the gospel must have an opportunity to hear and understand the gospel of Jesus Christ with its saving ordinances, and the opportunity to accept the gospel and receive the blessings of its saving ordinances before that great day when they must stand before the judgment bar of God to be judged for their own deeds in mortality. Since they missed this opportunity while living in mortality, they must receive the opportunity while in the world of spirits as they await the day of their resurrection. Otherwise, they could not be judged the same as those who had the opportunity to learn of Christ and his saving gospel while in mortality.

**"For for this cause was the gospel preached also to them that are dead, that they might be judged according to men in the flesh, but live according to God in the spirit." (1 Peter 4:6)**

Yes, the great plan of our Father provides a way for those who didn't hear and learn of and accept the gospel of Jesus Christ while here on the earth to have an opportunity to do so in the world of spirits while they await the day of their resurrection.

Christ foretold of this day when he would preach the gospel to the spirit world.

**"Verily, verily, I say unto you, The hour is coming, and now is, when the dead shall hear the voice of the Son of God: and they that hear shall live." (John 5: 25)**

Father's plan is beautiful and perfect. The gospel of Jesus Christ is preached in the spirit world for those who had no opportunity here on earth. Christ, in the short time he visited the world of spirits, while his physical body lay in the tomb, organized and commissioned a great missionary work among the righteous spirits there to take his saving gospel message to all in the spirit world **(See, D&C 138)**. All will have the opportunity to hear and understand the wonderful truths about God and about his plan for us, either here on earth or after their mortal death in the world of disembodied spirits while they await the day of their resurrection. They will all have an opportunity to accept or reject this great message of liberating truth, so that they may be **"judged according to men in the flesh,"** even though they continue to live as spirits until the day of their own resurrection.

Question: If **baptism** is a necessary step for one to be washed clean of his sins, (and we know that baptism is necessary; See, John 3:1-6; Mark 16:16; Acts 2:37-38) how can a disembodied spirit be baptized? The short answer is that it can't. How then may the spirit in the world of disembodied spirits who has accepted the truths of the gospel of Jesus Christ, demonstrated his faith, and repented of his own sins, how may he receive the blessings of baptism?

Unfortunately, little is said about this topic in the Bible as we have it. However, the Apostle Paul in his letter to the Corinthians, spoke of the early saints (members of the church of Jesus Christ) being **"baptized for the dead."** Paul spends much of his letter to the Corinthian saints trying to teach and convince them again of the reality of the resurrection. One of the arguments Paul uses to help the Corinthian saints see that there is indeed a resurrection is that he points out to them that members of the church are, in fact, being **"baptized for the dead."** He asks them, "if the dead rise not at all, why are they then baptized for the dead?"

**"Else what shall they do which are baptized for the dead, if the dead rise not at all? Why are they then baptized for the dead?" (1 Corinthians 15:29)**

Without doubt, more was understood and written by the early gospel writers about this doctrine of vicarious baptism by those living on behalf of the dead, a practice of the early members of the church clearly condoned by Paul. But it is clear that the church anciently understood this doctrine of vicarious baptisms for the dead, and practiced it. The sealing power of the priesthood, given to the apostles of old by Christ himself, allowed them to perform these ordinances on behalf of their kindred dead. (See, Matthew 16:19)

Since the sealing power of the priesthood has been restored again in these days with the restoration of the gospel, we may again bring the blessings of baptism and other priesthood ordinances to our kindred dead by performing these ordinances for them vicariously under the direction of the priesthood in temples of the Lord built for these purposes on the earth today. When we perform a baptism vicariously in a temple for one who is dead and who has accepted the gospel of Jesus Christ in the spirit world, the full blessings of the gospel become available to that repentant spirit, and then he may then be "judged according to men in the flesh" though he must continue to live in the spirit while he awaits the day of his resurrection.

The plan of our Father in heaven is truly a beautiful and perfect plan. It provides an opportunity for all to hear the gospel and to either accept or reject the saving truths for themselves. When the day of that great judgment comes, and we stand before our maker to be judged according to our works, none will be able to say that he didn't have a chance to take advantage of the saving ordinances of the gospel. Father's plan is infinitely fair, just, and merciful.

These teachings, my sweet children, are true. I bear my personal witness to you.

*Essay Nine*

## JESUS CHRIST IS JEHOVAH

To understand more correctly our relationship with our Lord Jesus Christ, it is necessary to understand the role of our Lord and Savior in the premortal world. As we know, Jesus Christ was the very first of the spirit offspring born of our Father in heaven. John referred to Christ as **"the beginning of the creation of God."** **(Revelation 3:14)** Paul referred to Jesus as the **"Firstbegotten"** **(Hebrews 1:6)** and referred to the Saints whose names are written in heaven as the **"church of the Firstborn."** **(Hebrews 12:23)**

The Apostle John clearly teaches that Jesus, or "the Word", existed with the Father from **"the Beginning,"** **(John 1:1-2)** meaning that Jesus' existence is co-eternal with the Father. Christ has been with the Father "from everlasting," or forever. There was never a time when Christ was not with the Father. This beautiful doctrine gives us added understanding of our own relationship with God, which is that we too have existed with the Father from the beginning. (See, ESSAY FOUR: OUR LIFE BEFORE OUR BIRTH INTO MORTALITY; supra, at pg 30*)*

Christ was the "Creator" of all things, under the direction of the Father. The Apostle John taught;

**"All things were made by him; and without him was not any thing made that was made." (John 1:3)**

Paul taught of Jesus Christ, the Son, that the Son was the instrumentality **"by whom also he** (meaning, the Father) **made the worlds;" (Hebrews 1:2)** It is interesting to note here that Paul refers to "worlds" in the plural, in speaking of the creations of the Father made through the instrumentality of Jesus Christ, the Son.

Before his mortal ministry, of course, Jesus Christ was still a spirit, without a body of flesh and bones, which he, like all of us, acquired upon his birth into mortality.

By understanding the role of Jesus Christ in the premortal creation of the earth, and of all other worlds also, the scripture in

Genesis takes on new meaning for us when it says in **verse 26 of Chapter 1 of Genesis**: **"And God said, Let _us_ make man in _our_ image, after _our_ likeness:"** God the Father was not alone when the earth and all things on it were created.

Practically all of the Father's dealings with his children here on earth have been through his Son, Jesus Christ. The God of the Old Testament, from the days of Moses, was referred to as the Great "I AM," or as "Jehovah." (Exodus 3:14) He who appeared to Moses in the burning bush, who brought the children of Israel out of Egypt and through the Red Sea, who gave the Ten Commandments to Moses on Mount Sinai, who followed the Israelites while in the wilderness by day in a pillar of a cloud and by night in a pillar of fire was Jehovah.

In the King James translation, Jehovah is rendered usually as **"THE LORD"** in small caps. The common, but erroneous assumption by modern readers is that the God of the Old Testament, the God of Abraham, Isaac, and Jacob, Jehovah, the Great I AM, is the "Father," when in fact those titles refer to "The Son, Jesus Christ."

The Apostle Paul repeatedly taught this great truth to the Saints of the early church that Jesus Christ was Jehovah of old. In his letter to the Corinthians, Paul wrote:

**"Moreover, brethren, I would not that ye should be ignorant, how that all our fathers were under the cloud, and all passed through the sea; And were all baptized unto Moses in the cloud and in the sea; And did all eat the same spiritual meat; and did all drink the same spiritual drink: for they drank of that spiritual Rock that followed them: and <u>that Rock was Christ</u>."** (1 Corinthians 10:1- 4)

In his letter to the Hebrews, Paul wrote:

**"By faith Moses, when he was come to years, refused to be called the son of Pharaoh's daughter; Choosing rather to suffer affliction with the people of God, than to enjoy the pleasures of sin for a season; <u>Esteeming the reproach of Christ</u> greater riches than the treasures in Egypt:"** (Hebrews 11:24-26)

Christ himself testified that he was the great **"I AM"** (John 8:58), the name given to Moses at the time of the burning bush for Moses to use to identify to the children of Israel the name of the God who spoke to Moses. The people in Christ's day clearly understood this reference to their God Jehovah and attempted to stone Jesus for blasphemy.

The Apostle John recorded Jesus' words when he said:

**"For had ye believed Moses, ye would have believed me: <u>for he wrote of me</u>." (John 5:46)**

When the risen Lord appeared to his followers in the Americas he announced to them:

**"Behold, I say unto you that the law is fulfilled that was given unto Moses. Behold, I am he that gave the law, and I am he who covenanted with my people Israel; therefore the law in me is fulfilled, for I have come to fulfill the law; therefore it hath an end." (3 Nephi 15:4-5)**

The words of the risen Lord to his prophet in this day again confirm his identity as the great **"I AM"** of old:

**"Listen to the voice of Jesus Christ, your Redeemer, the Great I AM, whose arm of mercy hath atoned for your sins;" (D&C 29:1;)**

Jehovah of old, the God of the Old Testament, the God of Abraham, Isaac and Jacob, the Great "I AM," the firstborn of our Father's spirit offspring, the only begotten of the Father in the flesh, the Promised Messiah, the Holy One, the Son of God, the Lamb of God, *is* Jesus Christ, the Savior and Redeemer of the world.

Of these precious truths, I bear to you, my sweet children, my personal and most solemn witness.

87

*Essay Ten*

## JUSTICE and PUNISHMENT
## MERCY and FORGIVENESS

Sin is the violation or transgression of God's law. Justice demands that there must be a consequence or punishment for every transgression of God's laws. God is Just. So, God's justice requires that every violation of his law cannot go unpunished. Because each of us from Adam on has sinned, justice requires that we suffer a punishment, part of which is that we are cut off from the presence of the Lord. Without some intervening act of Mercy, we would be forever cut off from the presence of the Lord.

The great blessing for us of the atonement of our Lord Jesus Christ is that Christ has taken upon Himself the punishment for each of our sins. In the very real sense He has purchased the debt that we owe to Justice by paying the debt for us with His own suffering and with his own precious blood. And since He now owns our debt, we are in His debt. Christ has, through his great atoning sacrifice, brought about the "Plan of Mercy" to appease the "demands of justice," that God might be both merciful and just. (Alma 42)

Christ's great plan of mercy is that He will forgive us of our sins if we will repent and keep His commandments. If we will repent and follow His commandments, Christ's mercy will claim us, and we will be spared the punishment of God's justice. The prophet Alma told his son Corianton: **"Therefore, O my son, whosoever will come may come and partake of the waters of life freely; and whosoever will not come the same is not compelled to come; but in the last day it shall be restored unto him according to his deeds." (Alma 42:27)**

Jesus Christ, because He was the only sinless and perfect man who ever lived, and because He was literally the Son of Almighty God in the flesh, was in the position to do what no other man could do. He alone had the accumulated "Grace" to be able to voluntarily substitute Himself for us, to suffer in our place the punishment for the sins we have committed so as to satisfy the demands of justice. He is our Savior. He is Just, yet He is merciful and kind. What He requires of us in order to be forgiven of our sins is to repent of our sins and to keep His commandments to the end of our life. If we will do this, He will mercifully forgive us, and we will be washed clean, as it were, by his precious blood.

The story is told of a particularly unruly class of students who ran off one teacher after another with their errant behavior. One new teacher who came into the class started by having the class as a whole determine a set of rules to govern their own behavior in the class, which they were more than happy to do. The class also decided that a punishment for anyone violating the class rules would be that the violator would be whipped with a small wooden rod a certain number of times across his bare back. Though the rules were much harsher than the teacher would have set for the class, the class unanimously voted to approve and accept the rules and the punishment they had arrived at for themselves. One day, the largest and roughest boy in the class complained very loudly that someone had stolen the sack lunch he had brought from home. The boy demanded that whoever stole the lunch should be beaten as the class rules required. After some investigation it was discovered that the lunch had been stolen by the smallest and frailest boy in the class. What was discovered was that the boy had no food at home and had taken the lunch because he was so very hungry. The class became very subdued when they discovered what had happened to the stolen lunch. The teacher, however, thought he had no alternative but to administer the punishment or completely loose the respect that the class had for their rules. The teacher brought the little frail boy up to the front of the class to administer the punishment. He insisted that the frail boy remove his coat to receive the beating. As the frail boy reluctantly removed his coat, the class saw that the little boy had no shirt on under his coat, and that he was so skinny all his ribs could be seen. As the class watched, the teacher reluctantly prepared to administer the requisite number of stripes to the frail boy's bare back. But before the teacher could start, the large rowdy boy whose lunch had been stolen stood up and asked the teacher was there anything in the class rules that prevented someone else from voluntarily taking the beating in the place of the person who was supposed to be punished. The teacher thought a moment and said, "No, there's nothing in the rules that would prevent that." So, the big, rough boy whose lunch had been stolen went up to the front of the class and took the beating in the place of the little frail boy.

Christ has taken our beating for us. With his stripes we are healed. (See, Isaiah 53:5) The Lord taught through his prophet Isaiah: **"Though your sins be as scarlet, they shall be as white as snow; though they be red like crimson, they shall be as wool." (Isaiah 1:18)**

Through his prophet Joseph Smith the Lord taught: **"Behold, he who has repented of his sins, the same is forgiven, and I, the Lord, remember them no more." (D&C 58:42)**

When I was a child, I heard a talk in which a man said that when we sin, it's like driving a nail into the back of a wooden door. He then said that when we repent, it's like the nail is pulled out, but the hole is still there. That bothered me until I realized that the man was completely wrong. When the Lord forgives us, it is as if the sin had never happened. There is no scar, no hole. The surface is pure and unmarred. It is true that we must deal with the consequences of our actions, but when the Lord forgives us, He remembers it **"no more."** We become as pure as the driven snow. And though our sins be terrible, or **"as scarlet,"** when the Lord forgives us, **"they shall be as white as snow."**

Christ pleads with us to come unto him and be healed. The prophet Alma taught: **"Behold, he sendeth an invitation unto all men, for the arms of mercy are extended towards them, and he saith: Repent, and I will receive you. Yea, he saith: Come unto me and ye shall partake of the fruit of the tree of life; yea, ye shall eat and drink of the bread and the waters of life freely;" (Alma 5:33-34)**

In speaking to us who will read the Book of Mormon, Moroni quoted the words of Isaiah: **"...Awake, and arise from** the dust...and put on thy beautiful garments..." (Moroni 10:31)

The Lord pleads with us to awake and arise from our sleep of indifference and slothfulness; to be cleansed from the soil of our iniquity through the atonement of our Savior by repentance and obedience to the laws of the Lord; to put on our works of righteousness; to shoulder the responsibility of the priesthood of God in helping to prepare the earth for the coming days of tribulation and glory incident to the second coming of our Lord.

While the principle of repentance and forgiveness is talked of in conjunction with the ordinance of baptism for a new convert, the great hope for all of us who have been baptized lies in the ability to continue to repent often of our sins, for it is only in this way that we can hope to be found clean before the Lord at the last day.

The steps to repentance are simple. Most importantly we must have a desire to change, a change in our heart, a change in the direction of our life. Certainly we must recognize the error in our actions, though I am convinced that our conscience, or the light of Christ in us, has told us already in our hearts what is right. And the needed change may be from an omission, or our failure to do something we know we should be doing.

Inherent in this process of repentance is that we must be humble enough to acknowledge and admit to ourselves and to our Father in heaven our need and desire to change, and our need and desire for His help. The simple act of turning to our Father in prayer, acknowledging from our heart to Him our need for change in our life, and asking for His help in changing our life will invoke the powers of heaven in our behalf. If we are truly humble, our Father will eagerly send His Spirit to strengthen us while we are yet a great way off from where we know we should be. We will feel and see in our life the love and tender mercies and hand of our Father in heaven as we humbly seek to change our life and come home to the loving out stretched arms of our Father, and the security of the saving truths of our Heavenly Father's plan.

The story told by Christ of the Pharisee and the publican, or the sinner, who both came to the temple to pray shows the great importance of a humble repentant attitude. The self-righteous Pharisee stood with outstretched arms and in a loud voice for all to hear thanked God that he was better than other men, while the publican stood afar off and would not so much as even lift up his eyes unto heaven, but smote upon his breast, saying, **"God be merciful to me a sinner."** And Christ taught: **"I tell you, this man [the publican] went down to his house justified** *rather* **than the other: for every one that exalteth himself shall be abased; and he that humbleth himself shall be exalted. (Luke 18: 10-14)**

Certainly we must show our Father our desire to change by forsaking that which we know is not pleasing in His sight, and fill that void with new energy directed at humble obedience to our Father's will. We show our change of heart, our repentance, by what we do. John the Baptist told the Pharisees and the Sadducees to bring forth fruits meet for repentance. (Matthew 3:7-8)

An important part of the repentance process must be for us to actually **_do_** the works of our Lord, that is, we must continue on our path toward Father's presence by doing the works of righteousness in our own life.

As we feel the desire to change and to come closer to Father, we will feel His Spirit within us urging and moving us on to overcome our natural tendencies and to live more righteously. We will also feel the desire and see opportunities to reach out to others around us to lift and encourage them also. Righteous works are a necessary and inevitable part of our path back home to the loving arms of our Savior.

A critical part of the repentance process is taught by our Lord in His parable of the ungrateful servant.

**"Therefore is the kingdom of heaven likened unto a certain king, which would take account of his servants.**

**And when he had begun to reckon, one was brought unto him, which owed him ten thousand talents.**

But forasmuch as he had not to pay, his lord commanded him to be sold, and his wife, and children, and all that he had, and payment to be made.

The servant therefore fell down, and worshipped him, saying, Lord, have patience with me, and I will pay thee all.

Then the lord of that servant was moved with compassion, and loosed him, and forgave him the debt.

But the same servant went out, and found one of his fellowservants, which owed him an hundred pence: and he laid hands on him, and took *him* by the throat, saying, Pay me that thou owest.

And his fellowservant fell down at his feet, and besought him, saying, Have patience with me, and I will pay thee all.

And he would not: but went and cast him into prison, till he should pay the debt.

So when his fellowservants saw what was done, they were very sorry, and came and told unto their lord all that was done.

Then his lord, after that he had called him, said unto him, O thou wicked servant, I forgave thee all that debt, because thou desiredst me:

Shouldest not thou also have had compassion on thy fellowservant, even as I had pity on thee?

And his lord was wroth, and delivered him to the tormentors, till he should pay all that was due unto him.

"So likewise shall my heavenly Father do also unto you, if ye from your hearts forgive not every one his brother their trespasses." (Matthew 18:23-35)

The bottom line is that for us to be forgiven by our Lord for the debt we owe to Him for our own sins, we must *from our hearts* forgive every one who has offended or sinned against us. There is no other way. We cannot carry a grudge or ill-feelings for others for their bad treatment of us, and then come to the mercy seat of our Savior and expect his compassion and mercy to forgive our debt and wash us clean when we have had no such compassion on others.

The risen Lord taught this same truth to the Nephites in the Americas as recorded in 3 Nephi 13; 14-15:

"**For, if ye forgive men their trespasses your heavenly Father will also forgive you;**

**But if ye forgive not men their trespasses neither will your Father forgive your trespasses.**" (3 Nephi 13: 14-15)

And again, the Lord has taught us in our day this sobering truth.

"**Wherefore, I say unto you, that ye ought to forgive one another; for he that forgiveth not his brother his trespasses standeth condemned before the Lord; for there remaineth in him the greater sin.**

**I, the Lord, will forgive whom I will forgive, but of you it is required to forgive all men.**" (D&C 64: 9-10)

Truly we must learn to have the same compassion and forgiveness for others as our Savior if we hope to become like Him and become "one" with He and our Father.

One of the greatest tools of the devil to keep captive those of us who are weighted down by the seeming enormity of our sins, is to convince us that we have gone astray too far, sinned too much to ever be able to repent and be forgiven again. The question was asked of the Master when one of his disciples kept faltering in his determination to keep the commandments. Peter asked the Lord, "**How oft shall my brother sin against me, and I forgive him? till seven times? Jesus saith unto him, I say not unto thee, Until seven times: but, Until seventy times seven.**" (Matthew 18:21-22)

The word of the Lord to his prophet Alma as recorded in the Book of Mormon makes very clear that the Lord will forgive us each time we repent with sincerity of heart.

"**... and if he confess his sins before thee and me, and repenteth in the sincerity of his heart, him shall ye forgive, and I will forgive him also. Yea, and as often as my people repent will I forgive them their trespasses against me.**" (Mosiah 26:29-30)

The prophet Moroni reconfirmed this same doctrine:

"**But as oft as they repented and sought forgiveness, with real intent, they were forgiven." Moroni 6: 8**

Please understand that the principle of repentance and forgiveness applies to all of us as we struggle through life's storms. The love of our Father and our Savior Jesus Christ for us is pure and absolute. All things are present before the Lord, the past and the future. He knows all. And yet He loved each of us from the beginning even though He knew we would commit the sins that we have committed. And He still loves us now even though we have committed such sins. His love for us is unconditional. Our salvation is His whole work and His whole glory. (See, Moses 1: 39)

Christ used the parable of the lost sheep to illustrate how important to Him is the one who has been lost. He said: **"What man of you, having an hundred sheep, if he lose one of them, doth not leave the ninety and nine in the wilderness, and go after that which is lost, until he find it? And when he hath found it, he layeth it on his shoulders, rejoicing." (Luke 15:4-5)** It is so remarkable to me to note that Christ, as the loving Good Shepard, places the lost sheep, who would certainly be dirty and full of briers and thistles in his wool, on his own shoulders and carries him home, rather than having the lost sheep follow behind on his own. I think this exemplifies the love and extra care that our Lord will give to us who have strayed and who in all humility desire to come back to him.

Then Christ told of the woman having ten pieces of silver, if she lose one piece, lights a candle, and sweeps the house, and seeks diligently till she finds it; and when she finds it she calls her friends and her neighbors together, saying, **"Rejoice with me; for I have found the piece which I had lost." (Luke 15:8-9)** Then Christ talks of the joy and rejoicing in heaven over one sinner that repenteth: **"Likewise, I say unto you, there is joy in the presence of the angels of God over one sinner that repenteth." (Luke 15:10)**

The crowning parable about the repentant soul is the story of the "prodigal son" which we all know. (Luke 15:11-32) The thing I want you to remember is that this is a story of a young man who had been raised by a good family with a knowledge of the truth.

When the prodigal had been sufficiently humbled by the buffetings of life, he turned toward home. He changed the direction of his life with the desire to go back home, back to the security of his father, back to what he knew was true. And, as the parable relates, while the returning son was yet a great way off his father saw him, and ran to meet him. This parable is symbolic for each of us as if we were in the shoes of the returning prodigal. While we are still a great way off from where we should be or need to be, our Father, because we have turned toward Him with a humble heart, asking His help, runs to meet us. And as in the parable of the returning prodigal, the Father had great compassion on his returning son. His heart was overflowing with joy. And he fell on his neck, and kissed him, and brought out his best robe and put it on him, and put a ring on his hand and shoes on his feet, and killed the fatted calf to feast and rejoiced. The Father's statement is very revealing: **"For this my son was dead, and is alive again; he was lost, and is found." (Luke 15:24)**

This shows us how our Savior will treat us as we, in humility and sincerity of heart, turn toward Him and move our life in the direction of what we know is true. Our Savior is waiting with open arms to receive us with love and compassion, beckoning to us to return and to drink freely from the waters of life. We only must humble ourselves and turn toward Him and away from the ways of the world.

I can assure you, my sweet children, that true happiness in life comes only by humble obedience to the will of our Father. We can rely on the tender mercies and patience and loving kindnesses of our loving Savior, Jesus Christ.

With His help and guidance, we must patiently and lovingly pull our children and loved ones close to us, using the example of our Savior himself, and teach them these saving truths so that together, as a family, we can return to the presence of our loving Savior and our Father in Heaven, and enjoy there the blessings of eternal life with our fathers who have gone before us and with our posterity who will come after. Of this I bear my most humble witness.

July30, 2008

www.ingramcontent.com/pod-product-compliance
Lightning Source LLC
Chambersburg PA
CBHW031409040426
42444CB00005B/490